THE ORPHAN OF GOD

A MEMOIR

❖ ❖ ❖

By

Pip Gordon

The day after the September 11th, 2001 attack on the World Trade Center in New York City, I walked into my Stagecraft classroom at Grinnell College to be met with absolute silence. I stood looking at anguished young adults coming to grips with the shock of their new reality. A slow hand raised to my left, my eyes blinked in recognition as his question landed on the lecture table.

"Professor Gordon," he asked, "Can you talk to us about hope?"

These are the moments when young hearts look toward old wisdom for solace. My answer came after a beat, a pause, a breath.

"Here, in this moment of time, I am looking at 27 reasons to hope. All of you are in college to become more educated, more compassionate and more understanding so that each of you can shape and grow your conviction to change and re-define your world."

This book is for those 27 students and the lesson of courage they taught me that day.

This story is an account of events, according to my memory. I have systematically changed the names of people and places. Some identifying characteristics have been altered to protect the privacy of those involved.

Scriptural verse used is from the King James translation of the Holy Bible; the official translation adopted by the Church of Jesus Christ of Latter Day Saints (Mormons).

CHAPTER 1

JOHN 15:12

*"This is my commandment,
That ye love one another,
as I have loved you."*

I hated my room. What had I done to be punished with such isolation from everyone else? I slowly climbed and counted each of the fifteen worn wooden treads of the long, vertical staircase to the upper hall lit by a solitary hanging bulb.

Last step.
Pause.
Breathe.
Turn left.
Reach for the small black metal toggle of the light switch.
Push up to turn off the hall light.
Darkness.
Focus.
My room had no light.
Run for cover under the eiderdown strewn across my unmade bed.
Wait for the shadows.
Wait for the noises.
Wait for sleep to come.

I desperately hoped I would not wake up in the night to go to the toilet. The toilet was another mile away past the railing banisters and pitfalls of the upper landing that skirted the stairwell. All of my precious toys had met their death by being thrown over the edge by my brothers so I knew it was dangerous territory.

My brothers' seemed to be forever away. Their room was lined by two bunk beds and two dressers separated by a lioness skin that hugged the floor. She was shot in South Africa by my grandfather. Now she lay in the center of the room in New Zealand with her large heavy head resting on the floor. My

fingers often played with her long ivory teeth and when my brothers were at
Sunday-morning-boys-only-church, I would lay the length of her to gently
run my hands up and down the ridge of her back.

> "Where were you when you heard the bolt pull back?" I
> whisper.
> "In the brilliance of savanna light, resting with my chil-
> dren," she says.
> "Will you miss them when it comes?" I ask.
> "They will know how to hide in their shade."

I stretch my reach to fit my small hand in hers. Her strong claws spread my
fingers wide. My head rests softly and perfectly in the hug of her neck. We
lay in the morning sun splayed together on the bedroom floor.

> "I'm going to be strong like you when I grow up."
> "Be careful where you step," she whispers.
> "Can your legs carry me?"
> "Where do you want to go?" she asks.
> "With you."

My hand reaches around to stroke her soft face. My fingertips find wide
marble eyes and brush her delicate ears as she rests easy on her chin. I
twirl her hair down to her flanks broad and brown. My little finger finds
the hole in her skin where the bullet ripped open her lion heart.

> "Did it sting when the burn drilled into your flesh?"

In the silence of our space, she never talks to me about the hurt.

My parent's bedroom was off limits. Storms always happened in their
room so I learned never to go there. One such night ocean winds moved
the shadows on my wall as the metal drainpipe slapped hard against the
outside of my window.
Bang! I awoke.
The yelling was loud.

The storm was loud.

Was it in my dream or out of my dream?

It was down the hall. In fright I ran from the darkness to my parents' room and threw open the door. More yelling.

A shoe flew across the room and bounced off the door.

I ducked.

Mother had never thrown a shoe at me before.

What had I done?

Standing at the end of the bed my father glared at me with such intensity his eyes pushed me back and pressed my back into the edge of the banister. Mother started toward me. A whoosh of air passed my face as the door slammed shut. I ran back to my room knowing it must have been my fault.

A few days earlier I had been sent to brush my teeth in the small downstairs bathroom. Looking at the glass full of upside down toothbrushes, I could not remember which one could possibly be mine. I chose the yellow one and went into the living room to ask Daddy if the yellow one was mine.

> "Is this my toothbrush?" I asked.

My father was sitting in his chair with a guitar on his lap. A tall glass of milk and a bottle of vodka sat between the chair leg and his feet. His pointing finger pushed me back.

> "No! Don't ever use that toothbrush! I'll have your guts for garters if you've used that toothbrush! That's my toothbrush! Put it back where you found it and never touch it again!" he shouted.

I ran back to the high sink, placed the yellow toothbrush back into the glass and made the long run up the stairs to the darkness of my room and the cover of my eiderdown.

Now days later and in the middle of the night they were fighting about it. Everything could be better if he would just give me a minute to tell them that I had not actually used that toothbrush – ever! I did not even touch the white bristles that go in your mouth. I did not put any of my germs on it. I was only confused for a little moment because there were too many colors in the glass and I never remembered which color was just for me.

The yelling was louder.
Stomping in the hallway.
More yelling.
Fifteen very loud footsteps stomped down the staircase.
Fifteen more.
My parents had gone down to the kitchen.
Doors slammed.
Silverware crashed to the kitchen floor.

Surely my brothers had heard the commotion. Hugging the wall side of the hallway, I ran to their bedroom, opened the door and flung myself onto the back of my lion. All three brothers were out of bed. Lightning and storm showed the outline of their pajamas against the windowpanes of the balcony where they had their faces pressed to the glass. I nudged my way through and pressed my face to the cold.

It was raining hard.
We all heard the car start.
It was Daddy.
He was going somewhere in the middle of the night.
The headlights turned on.
The windscreen wipers turned on.
All at once the car revved up and raced up the hill and out of the driveway. As he sped down the street we lost sight of him in the storm and in the darkness.

It was 1961.
I was five years old and I never saw my father again.

Chapter 2

*"Blessed are the peacemakers,
for they shall be called the children of God."*

My father, Peter Albert Thomas Gordon was groomed to follow in his father's footsteps. After all, the Gordon men had been notable Irish surgeons and my father was to be no exception. The problem was that he was more interested in sailing yachts and riding motorcycles than embracing the textbook discipline to become a doctor. Schooled at Epsom College in London, he knew enough to view the medical profession as too dull and far too demanding. My father desired adventure, travel, and most of all, to pursue a life at sea that would provide some relief from his overly protective mother and land-loving, boorish stepfather.

Before the family knew enough to stop him, Peter had lied about his age to get his uniform and his acceptance into the British merchant navy as an apprentice gunner. Leaving home at the age of seventeen his passion was now his duty to King and country and to the boundless horizons and the salt laden air of the ocean. Peter left by train for Liverpool and immediately upon arrival was assigned to the ten thousand ton merchant ship *Dorset* under the command of Captain Tuckett. The *Dorset* was commissioned by the British merchant navy from The New Zealand Shipping Company and was put into service delivering food supplies and stores to rationed and embattled England. The ship would traverse enemy infested supply routes through the treacherous north seas of the Atlantic Ocean between Liverpool and New York, down the American east coast, through the Panama Canal and then south, across the Pacific Ocean to Australia and New Zealand.

Conveniently, family admonishment and guilt came only through the postal service when Peter was in safe harbor for mail deliveries. On one such occasion ashore in New Zealand, he pulled out of his mailbag a small gold edged card inscribed with,

*'The Wellington New Zealand Benevolent Society invites you
to an evening of entertainment and dance to be held at the
Wellington Town Hall, Saturday May 28th, 1941.'*

New Zealander's were renowned for their hospitality to the many British and American servicemen that found rest and refuge on her shores. Delighted at the invitation, Peter and his shipmates gleefully saw it as their duty to attend. To do otherwise would certainly seem ungrateful and would mean a missed opportunity to change out of their crusty cotton uniforms into their dress blues. To do otherwise also meant passing up one of the few opportunities in a long war to socialize with the opposite sex.

Handsome and fresh, pressed and polished, it wasn't too long into the festivities when Peter was introduced to a twenty-one year old society girl named Harriet Stanton Ray, daughter of Jeremy and Lenore Ray. Strikingly beautiful, Harriet was a picture of elegant perfection standing in her designed ballroom gown, smart shoes, coifed honey-blonde hair, twinkling blue eyes and warm, welcoming smile. It was no surprise that her dance card was becoming quite full of visiting American and British sailors and a string of local New Zealand suitors.

Charming and endowed with little patience Peter asked Harriet to dance. Throughout the evening and often in mid step, maneuvers began. Harriet was ready for the chase. Wellington Girls College had prepared her well. Equipped with lessons in Latin, drama, music, geography, arithmetic, conversation, and a sporting game of tennis, she was always perfectly engaging. Dance partners changed as often as a tap on the shoulder. Peter frequently cut in to sweep Harriet off her dance floor feet. Compliments of navy blue and white twirled around the room in a fox trot. In motion, flashes of smiles and intense stares ignited the fuse of a fast burning romance that only the desperation of war could fuel. The moment the evening was over, the relationship became a regimen of writing, port visits, long days at sea, weeks of silence, more letters and cable telegrams, more waiting and more wanting.

Five months after their eyes meeting, Peter's ship *Dorset* had been ordered to join *Operation Pedestal*, the last and largest convoy sent by Churchill to break the German siege of Malta. A small island in the Mediterranean, Malta was deemed a strategic necessity as an allied refueling depot and landing strip for fighters and allied bombers. Securing the island was critical to the successful defeat of Rommel's advancing German army in the North Africa campaign. By the late summer of 1942, the people of Malta were starving and in desperate need of all the supplies the merchant ships could carry. The British planes stood idle in need of all the aircraft fuel each ship was assigned to carry.

By August 27th, 1942 only seven of the twenty-nine merchant ships were within one hundred miles of Malta. One by one each ship was blown out of the water, set afire or torpedoed without warning in the middle of the night. In a strategic run for cover and pulling away from the main convoy to draw enemy fire, the *Dorset*, now without destroyer protection, was under constant air attack by waves of Italian bombers while dodging wolf packs of the infamous German U-boats.

Peter never left his mid-ship Balfor gun. After three days and nights of coffee, ham sandwiches and a continuous blistering air assault, four bombs exploded so close to the *Dorset* that the entire hull momentarily, and literally, lifted out of the water. A wall of water hit Peter and his gunner's mate, throwing them out of their high mid-ship turret onto the deck twelve feet below. Shaking off the shock of the fall and the cold Mediterranean Sea, they each struggled to climb back up to the turret to continue firing at any menacing Italian fighter while their eyes pierced through white capped waves in wait of a German torpedo. The force of the Italian bombs exploding in the water ripped open rivets and steel on impact.

"Abandon ship! All hands, abandon ship!"

The ship shuddered badly to starboard as Captain Tuckett's voice pierced through the ship's intercom and the roar of the flames as aircraft fuel burned all around them.

"All hands, all hands. Release the rafts. Release the rafts. Lower starboard lifeboats! Lower starboard lifebo-"

The crackle of the intercom cut out as the sea consumed generators in the lower decks. Explosions ripped the sidewall out of hold number four. Number four hold stored the *Dorset's* entire ration of aircraft fuel.

It is astonishing to know of the staggering number of merchant seamen lost at sea in World War II and equally astonishing to know how many English merchant seamen went to sea despite their inability to swim. It was common knowledge that the odds of survival if thrown into the sea were slim to none. Kapok life vests became weights after long hours in the water. Hypothermia came quickly in the cold Atlantic and sharks came mercilessly in the warm Pacific. Enemy ships would run through survivors floating in the sea and enemy planes would machine gun seamen adrift to deflate Allied morale. The survival of merchant seamen in the water depended solely on the availability of nearby allied ships to change course and find men alive floating amongst the oil, the bodies and the debris.

"Grab the winch, grab the winch! Eight in the boat, eight in the boat!" yelled the first mate as the wooden lifeboat scraped down the steel, listing hull to the ocean below. "Watch the line, watch the line! More slack on the forward line!" he screamed to the midshipman at the control.

At once the lifeboat came to a jarring tilt joined by the screaming grind of snapped and twisted cable racing through the smoking winch. The boat suddenly released and slapped down hard on the ocean surface throwing eight men into the sea. Flailing in their kapok and canvas life vests each man desperately grabbed for other helping hands to drag each other into the boat. Tangled cable cascaded from the ships winch system and now draped the gunnels of their only hope of survival.

> "Number two, number two," screamed the first mate, "engage the propeller, engage the propeller!"

Nothing.
No whir to be heard.
No sound of a motor.
No churn of the water.
Only the sound of a burning sea; of writhing hot steel and the screaming silence of eight oil-covered faces of terror.

Back on the calm shores of New Zealand, the wait for men had become a familiar theme in Harriet's family. After all, her mother Lenore had waited to marry her husband through an eight-year courtship that spanned the same oceans. A talented pianist, Lenore left New Zealand at the age of seventeen to continue her piano studies at the Wagner Conservatory in Berlin, Germany. Sailing with her piano teacher and chaperone, Lenore met the glance of a young engineer, Jeremy Ray. It was lust at first sight and the sly and swift passing of notes to each other as they passed through the narrow passageways in the bowels of the ship. The excitement of a touch, a look, was all it took to keep her feelings of seasickness and fright of the stormy, unrelenting Atlantic waves at bay. As with her daughter Harriet, the moment Lenore disembarked the correspondence began. But that was then, a great war and a generation ago. Harriet could be as determined and as patient; especially with a man whose charm she could conjure in her memory in an instant as she read his letters between long months punctuated by sporadic twenty-four hour shore leaves.

> *Dearest Harriet,*
>
> *We are on our forty-second day and skies are clear and gulls circle the ship in happiness to find a place to rest from flight. I am missing you with each beat of their wings, wishing I could fly*

like the gulls to New Zealand shores to dance once more and talk about things that matter.

I received a cablegram from Mother to say that you are most welcome to stay in London and that she would arrange passage if you would agree to come. Please come. I will have shore leave in two months once we dock in Liverpool. We work hard to maintain some semblance of normalcy by fishing when we have the time. Ian and I managed to catch a small shark that gave us a good fight on the line. Shark meat is very tasty and cook made a meal of it that night which was a welcome relief from our rations.

I miss your lemon meringue pie and your wonderful butter biscuit crust. I miss your hold. I taped the photo you sent to the outside of my storage cupboard at the foot of my bunk. Every night I miss everything about you. Every day I miss everything about you.

Please tell your parents not to worry too much. We will find safe harbor and I will be in the warmth of your arms as soon as the King and the navy will allow it.

Affectionately
Peter

The *Dorset* was alone and sinking one hundred miles northwest of Malta. Thirty miles away, the nearest allied ship was under U-boat and air attack.

Eight men in a lifeboat.

Eight men in the middle of hell.

"Number two, Number two, engage the propeller!" repeated the first mate as the second mate reached for the mechanized gear lever to start the propeller. The shaft failed to turn.

"Check the battery packs! Forward compartment! Forward compartment!" yelled the first mate over the groan of twisting steel.

The *Dorset* lifeboat was quickly being pulled toward the sinking hull. Fire had consumed the upper decks of the ship and was creeping toward the gelatinous oil slick slowly fingering toward the small craft. Drowning would be a merciful death compared to burning alive on a floating pyre.

> "Battery dry, battery dry!" bellowed number two, "it has to be below!" he shouted as his eyes searched above the water line for evident compromises to the motor system.

It could only be something wrong under the boat. Perhaps they had fouled the steel cables still dragging under the water from the winch rigging. Perhaps the shaft had been bent by the impact of the fall. The small boat was unable to move far from the suction of the soon-to-be rolling ship and was drifting dangerously closer to the floating islands of burning fuel; someone had to shed his life jacket to swim under the boat and take a look.

> "Who can swim? Who can swim?" screamed the second mate in an unabashed state of panic.

At the stern, an oil-covered hand shot quickly up into the air. It belonged to a broad shouldered youngster whose intense blue eyes pierced through the black grime covering his face.

> "Seaman, clear the foul under the boat! Check the stern! Check the shaft! Check the propeller! Something is jamming the propeller!!" cried the second mate.

Pulling off his kapok vest, discarding water-heavy socks and boots, the lad dove into the sea. Swimming hard, he began feeling his way across the bottom of the boat. He could feel the winch cables tightly wrapped around the propeller shaft. He gripped the stressed cable and began to unwind it from its paralyzing hold. Frayed wire cable cut deep into his hands. Lack of breath shot him back to the surface, gulping for relief. Salt water, aircraft fuel and oil burned down his throat into his stomach. He vomited in the water, took a deep breath and disappeared under the boat to finish the task. Gasping for air he resurfaced coughing and choking on vomit as two sailors heft him over the side and beached him squarely in the bottom of the boat.

"Gear lever down, gear lever down!" came the command.

The whine of the propeller immediately started to turn, pushing the lifeboat and its cargo of men away from the fiery, sinking *Dorset*. Shivering in his oil-soaked cotton khakis, the young man with fearless intensity sat upright with raw, bloodied, salt water stinging hands, clinging to the wooden gunnels of the boat. With his shirt torn open and his grazed arms spread wide, fire lit waters caught the glint of a small chain dangling against his hairless chest. At the end of the chain hung what appeared to be a delicate ring. It had been around his neck from the moment battle stations were called.
It was Midshipman Peter Albert Thomas Gordon's only possession.
Precious white gold now covered in black oil.
It was an engagement ring for Harriet.

After three scorching days and cold harrowing nights adrift, the men were relieved to be finally plucked from the sea by the search and rescue destroyer *HMS Bantham*, one of only four ships out of twenty-nine that sailed into Grand Harbor to break the siege of Malta. Once on dry land, my father immediately telephoned his mother, Carol Gailbraith, in London, assuring her that he was safe and well. More cablegrams were dispatched to other members of the family, and to Harriet:

*'Peter Safe And Well Lost Everything Cable
When Home Love Carol Gailbraith'.*

Naval headquarters in Valletta, Malta also sent cablegrams to London where newspaper wires hummed with the news of victory and defeat. News of his heroic deeds also made the headlines in the *London Evening News*:

'For 4 Days He Stuck To His Gun – But He Didn't Tell His Mother'

His hometown newspaper headline read:

'Bravery at Sea – Bromley Youth'

In New Zealand, the newspaper in Wellington featured the heroic story:

"Engagement Ring Carried Through Battle!"

My father received the Lloyds Medal for Bravery awarded to apprentice gunners and the Distinguished Service Medal from King George VI of England at Buckingham Palace. Harriet sailed immediately for London. With a monetary gift of four hundred pounds and the gift of a one-month leave, my father booked passage on a ship bound for America. With Harriet at his side, they celebrated their engagement by sailing through forty-foot waves in blackout conditions through the U-boat-infested North Atlantic towards the protection of the gentle swell of New York harbor.

He knew Harriet loved the theatre and he was very happy to oblige her appetite for it. They attended every show there was to see on Broadway. The rest of the four hundred pounds was spent on tasty American food, American nylon stockings, American cigarettes and living as if there might never be another tomorrow. Returning to England and with all parents present they were married in a small country church followed by a beautiful garden party reception with all the table trimmings fit for the hero and his lovely bride.

It was 1943 and my father was barely twenty-one years old.

CHAPTER 3

MATTHEW 6:24

*"No man can serve two masters; for either
he will hate the one, and love the other;
or else he will hold to the one, and
despise the other..."*

With no time for a honeymoon, my parents returned to serve the war effort. My father went back to sea on the merchant ship *Penton*. My mother signed up for the London Women's Observer Corps, a job that entailed long hours of looking skyward through binoculars to spot German bombers, fighters, V1 and V2 rockets on their way to destroy London. The in-laws protested. The job was far too dangerous for the wife and caretaker of their son and as such they arranged to have her join the London branch of the Army Corps Post Office, sorting and re-routing mail headed for the troops in Europe and North Africa.

Danger was not averted, however. Screaming fighter planes, dog fights and machine gun fire overhead, the thunderous din of Lancaster bombers at low altitude, the high pitch sirens and clanging bells of fire brigades, the rubble in the streets and the breaking shriek of nightly air raid sirens were all sounds of the blitz, the battle being fought for king and country over the skies of London. Those were the days and nights when my mother wished she were safe in the tranquility of her New Zealand home where wisteria grew oh so slowly up the trellis and the scent of lavender and roses permeated window screens on the southern breeze and soothing calm of summer.

Living with her in-laws in London was just as nerve-racking as living with the war. Mother was always under the scrutiny of the ever watchful and critical eyes of Carol, my grandmother, who was intent on teaching Harriet exactly how to iron, fold, launder and hang the clothes of my father and Carol's only son. Also on her agenda was to have Harriet learn how to cook a dull and colorless English breakfast of blood sausage, poached eggs and toast exactly as Peter would have it. Simply, my mother was being kept in storage and meticulously groomed to become the perfect wife until my father's return from duty.

Two years later and standing with thousands of war weary Brits in Trafalgar Square, London, my mother celebrated V-Day with King and country, commonwealth and relief. My father finally returned from service matured and battle weary bearing the weight of two demanding mistresses, my mother and the sea. He also bore the pain of chronic stomach ulcers from swallowing aircraft fuel and oil in the waters northwest of Malta. There was little he could do about it. Drinking milk would help line and soothe his stomach. Drinking vodka would help soothe his nerves. Needing to support his young wife and with the war now over, he signed on with the merchant marine and was shipped out to Liverpool. By 1946 first daughter and my big sister Rebecca was born.

The next year they relocated half way around the world to South Africa, the first move of many enabling my father to work toward the rank of Captain. My mother was always well-mannered, devoutly Anglican, stoic, stubborn, proud and loyal. Traveling from New Zealand to meet Peter in London was one thing but to be transplanted to the unfamiliar African landscape and language without any family support system was terrifying. Being alone and a minority was something to which Harriet was not accustomed. She had lived with her parents until the age of 23 and was used to familial surrounds and support. Her time in England although strained was still within familial walls, albeit a family she had to learn to love. As my father was at sea for six months at a time on the Cape Town to Liverpool shipping route, Harriet was left to care for Rebecca and now a second newborn daughter named Gylian.

Like Rebecca, Gylian was a red headed fair skinned beautiful child with perfect form and old soul blue eyes. Chubby rounded creamy white flesh lay on baby blankets under the warm African sun. Long days alone became consumed with tending two infants, washing and ironing baby linens and clothing and when the peace of night came any time left was consumed by writing letters to my father to bring connection from his rolling sea to the front stoop of her small brick apartment on a dusty dirt road in Cape Town, South Africa. Beyond the loneliness of the southern sky my parents would look at the same moon thousands of miles apart and the girls would look at each other with glee as they played and rolled around on the living room floor.

> "Hello, Cape Town Hospital Emergency Service. How can I help you?" the nurse said in the monotonous tone she had practiced in a lifetime of answering the phone.
> "Hello, this is Mrs. Harriet Gordon. My child is in distress – she has a temperature and her skin looks to have a rash. I'm wondering if I should bring her to the hospital."
> "Mrs. Gordon what is the name of your child?" the nurse asks as the rattle of paper scratched across the phone lines.
> "Gylian" my mother holds the young baby while Harriet speaks into the large black receiver.
> "Age?" asks the nurse.
> "Ten months, almost eleven months. I don't know what to do as she seems to be having a difficult time breathing," Harriet's voice raises in pitch as anxiety begins to surface.
> "Can you bring her to the hospital?" the nurse asks.
> "No I am so sorry that I cannot. I do not have an automobile and I have another child in the flat so I can't leave." Harriet's voice is now raised in acceptance of the fact that her baby is sick and she has no means to get her the help she desperately needs.
> "I am sending an ambulance right away. Stay on the telephone while I get the driver for directions."

With Rebecca in one arm and hope in the other, Mother sat for hours on a hard wooden bench in a hospital corridor while doctors ran test after test to see what Gylian's condition could be. After several blood tests she was diagnosed with a kidney disorder; it would be several days before doctors would get her infection under control. Mother returned to her flat with little Rebecca where she would wait for the phone to ring.

Eleven hours later.
Harriet reached for the phone in the telephone nook to stop the bell ringing.

> "Hello" she said.
> "Hello, Mrs. Gordon?" came an accented Afrikaans male voice on the line.
> "Yes, this is she," Harriet nervously replied.
> "Ah, yes then, well ahem yes. Um, Mrs. Gordon, This is Doctor Breivik from Cape Town General - "
> "Yes Doctor Breivik," Harriet said interrupting his stutter in anticipation that he was calling to tell her to come and bring Gylian home.
> "I am sorry to inform you that there was nothing that we could do to stop the infection. We did all that we knew how to do. I'm very, very sorry but we lost Gylian early this morning. If you would please call the morgue you will be able to make the arrangements for burial with the nurse on duty. Again Mrs. Gordon, we are so sorry for your loss."

Silence.
Breathing on the phone line.
The sounds of rustling paper and office voices unsettled the silence.

> "Thank you Doctor," a wisp of a voice replied.

Harriet ever so slowly placed the black phone on the silver receiver hooks and leaned hard against the wall. Knees buckling, body shaking she slid slowly down to the floor. Silent anguish squeaked out between her teeth. Tears stung her face.
Gylian had died.
Gylian had died alone.
Gylian had died of kidney disease two months shy of her first birthday.

With the assistance of the hospital staff, my mother made the necessary arrangements for Gylian to be buried without ceremony at the Cape

Town Cemetery. At home with Rebecca she was unable to go out and unable to reach out. She was at home, a young mother of a dead child. She was at home in an unfamiliar land. She was alone to conjure simple explanations and lies about death and heaven to her three-year-old Rebecca.

My father, sailing and en-route from New York harbor, refused emergency transport to get to Cape Town any sooner than was originally scheduled. The ultimate pragmatist, he knew there was nothing to be done. Getting to Cape Town any faster would not bring his Gylian back from the dead. Standing on deck in the cradle of the sea my father shared his grief amid the frigid winds and roll of white-capped waves of the unrelenting Atlantic Ocean. My mother shared her grief with no one.

Knock, knock, knock!
With Rebecca clinging to her skirt Harriet opened the front door to face two very young Americans standing in the frame.

> "Good morning. We represent the Church of Jesus Christ of Latter-day Saints. We have an important message for you and your family. May we come in to share this message from your Heavenly Father with you?"

Mormon missionaries have a very distinctive look. Always in twos, they peddle their message of salvation, wearing bright white shirts, muted ties, dark two-piece suits, shiny black shoes; they have ultra white teeth, clean-shaven faces, short-cropped hair and zealous soul-saving smiles. Like most salesmen, they are well trained with visual aids and flip charts, well trained in rejection, well trained in planning strategies, and most of all well trained to be systematically persistent.

One month after the death of my sister Gylian, the Mormon missionaries had made sure my mother was one of their regular stops as she pulled away from her beliefs in the Church of England and towards the enticing newness and fellowship of Mormonism. By the time my father returned from his six months at sea, my mother, Harriet Stanton Ray Gordon had been baptized into the Mormon Church by full immersion in an indoor swimming pool in Cape Town, South Africa, by a wholesome, white, young Mormon missionary from America.

My father wanted nothing to do with the Mormon Church.
He saw it as an American cult and would not be convinced otherwise.
His relationship with my mother became strained.
Both made concessions.

While he was ashore, she would limit her church activities to attending one meeting on Sunday. She tolerated his smoking and drinking even as her coffee, tea and wine drinking ceased. She would say her prayers three times a day in the privacy of the bathroom and would silently bless the food on the table before she ate. He was aware of the mutterings but said nothing in the hope this fad would lose its appeal once she realized it was an American cult. Visits by the missionaries were cordial, but few. While my father was at sea, the church again became the very center of my mother's activities and social calendar. The Church of England had never kept her so busy. Now she had Mormon meetings and visits at least five times a week and not a moment to spare on a thought of the loss of Gylian or the loneliness of being a young mother and the wife of a man who was never home.

Rebelling against her upbringing in the Church of England was never discussed despite the verbal dismay and concern from both parents and her in-laws. Raising a young family and serving her husband was delicately balanced with secluded scripture study and silent prayer. She learned that loving one another was not the only commandment required for salvation. Her demeanor shifted to one of quiet determination coupled with the unwavering righteousness of knowing that her Mormon religion was the only way, the only truth and the only path to eternal life.

Hoping that a change of location would end my mother's fascination with all things American, my father demanded they moved back to England. She dutifully obeyed. While in Liverpool, their first son, Jeremy Thomas Gordon was born. Moving again for promotion, this time to Wellington, New Zealand, my father completed his requirements to be first mate with The New Zealand Shipping Company. My mother was at last only forty miles away from her aging parents and happy to be home in her beloved Wellington. Second son Cedric Gailbraith Thomas Gordon was born. Three years later – twins! Rodney Gordon was born and thirty minutes later a daughter.

It was May 1956. I was named Philippa.

Five years later and with five children under the age of fourteen, my father, Peter Albert Thomas Gordon, finally left my mother. Events surrounding his departure were salted with Mormon insistence that my mother's salvation was hindered by my father's unwillingness to join the church. Bishops and brethren tried with all their might to convert him to Mormonism. My mother became more and more demanding of a spiritual commitment. They argued loudly and spent days apart. Divorce was strongly encouraged and finally mandated by the Mormon brethren who informed my mother that separation from my father was spiritually required if my mother was to progress towards the Celestial and highest Mormon kingdom of heaven. She believed them.

There was also another woman in the picture which supported the assertion that my father was a stereotypical, philandering, seafaring rogue, complete with "a woman in every port". Edith McKay was her name and she lived in a small flat in Auckland, New Zealand. My father would spend much time there to find safe harbor from the demands of five children and the religious battering waiting for him at home. The months at sea were no longer long enough and refuge at home was not possible. Always the Captain of his ship, my father looked at his options – land or sea, him or them, God or guts, anchor or sail, stay or leave, now or then.

Sea.
Him.
Guts.
Sail.
Leave.
Now.

Twenty years of moving and marriage.
Six children. One dead.
A petition filed for divorce.

The fact was that although they had endured a bloody war, horrific heart-
break and the vigil and vastness of two oceans, my parent's twenty-year
marriage was over. The fact also was that the doctrine of the Mormon
Church provided the impetus through spoken repeated spiritual
demands for our family to break apart.

CHAPTER 4

MATTHEW 5:48

"Be ye therefore perfect, even as your Father which is in heaven is perfect."

I knew a lot when I was five.
I was in Primer One and Mrs. Cheverton was my teacher.
She was really old! Her hands were wrinkly, and sometimes they would shake. Most days at school they shook at me.

> "Philippa!" she screeched.
> "Yes, Mrs. Cheverton," I answered with my no-body voice.
> "Philippa, I said no noise! Five minutes in the kennel!" she said with her boney finger point.

Only bad people were sent to the dog kennel, a large cardboard box that sat in the corner of the classroom. A small opening sat at the front of the box and darkness sat at the back. Donald Busfield was often in the dog kennel because he couldn't be quiet during naptime. Donald also cried a lot and needed a handkerchief pinned to his cardigan so he could blow his nose. My twin brother Rodney was so silent he never blew his nose and he never had to go to the dog kennel.
I was always in the dog kennel.

Sitting in the back corner next to the darkness my eyes searched for light slivers that quietly crept under the folds of the cardboard lid while my fingers searched the air for their glow. My feet searched for the push against the sides of the box. My heart searched for nothing. My mind searched for the stories I had come to know every Saturday morning on the radio. *Flick* the little fire engine, *Little Toot* the tugboat, courageous *Kiwi* and the *Little Engine that Could*. I tried not to think of poor little *Koala* and I never thought of my Dad.

Flick's song played loud in my head and would often sneak out of the
corner of my mouth,

> *"...I'm a little fire engine, Flick is my name, they won't let me
> put out fires, isn't that a shame! One day I'll be strong enough
> to fight every flame, call the little engine, call the little engine,
> I'm the little engine, Flick..."*

> "Five more minutes!" bellowed Mrs. Cheverton from the
> classroom light beyond the box.

Flick ignored her and so did I.

Little Toot was in the dog kennel with me all the time. He would toot
his little horn in the harbor with all the other big tugboats. One day he
tooted the wrong toot and got into big trouble! When bad things happened Mother tugboat would always sing,

> *"...Won't you ever grow up Little Toot? Won't you ever grow
> up Little Toot."*

She would then teach him the right toot over and over so he could safely
push and pull the big boats. Little Toot grew up to be Master Tugboat
in the harbor so I knew I could be a Master Tugboat too if I learned his
songs and practiced the right toots.

Mrs. Cheverton never ever mentioned tugboats, so I knew she didn't
know about Little Toot. If she did, she would have known that I did not
deserve to be in the dog kennel. I began to mumble my troubles to the
back of the cardboard wall.

> "Philippa! No talking! You will be in there all day if you
> don't stop talking," spat Mrs. Cheverton as she hit the
> blackboard hard with white chalk.

Oh dear, Mrs. Cheverton was getting mad. Maybe she would get so mad
she would take my voice away.

Moon had taken little Koala's voice away. Like Mrs. Cheverton, Moon had warned Koala to be quiet but Koala could not help himself. He boasted to Moon that he could beat her in a race to the next valley. Like Mrs. Cheverton, Moon was in no mood to be patient. She agreed to race him knowing that her light would always win. Determined little Koala raced as hard as he could by jumping like the wind from tree to tree. But Koala was not fast enough to beat the light of the moon to the next valley and lost the race.

> "Little Koala," said Moon to all in the sky who could hear, "Do you not know how fast my light can travel, do you not see the reach of my power, do you not understand that because you were boastful you will be silenced!"
> "Please no, please no," pleaded Koala until his voice became one with the trees.

Moon took his voice away and forever more, Koala would never speak to the wind.
Koala should not have been so boastful.
Moon should not have been so mean!
Koala should not have said anything.
He should be quiet. Just keep quiet!
I learned to keep away from the moon for it was that same moon that made the scary shadows in my bedroom. It was that same moon that pulled my father out to sea.

The dark corner of the dog kennel never felt safe and naptime never seemed to be done. Mrs. Cheverton was being mean. I told myself to keep quiet over and over again. "She's lucky she isn't a bird in the forest," I muttered to myself. She sort of looked like a bird sometimes. Her collar would be fluffy and she wore dresses that were bright and patterned like leaves, or feathers. Boney legs and old lady shoes made her shuffle in scratchy, stiff little jerks across the wooden floor. She was just one, mean, knobby-kneed bird! For a moment in my whispers I wished it were true.

If she were a bird in the forest, she would have to answer to Tane, the great Maori God of the Forest. Tane was much taller than Mrs. Cheverton. One day, Tane asked Tui bird to go down to the forest floor to eat the worms and grubs. The insects were making the beloved Kauri trees, the greatest and tallest trees of the forest, very sick.

Tui was scared of the dark and said "No".

Tane asked Pukeko bird.

Pukeko did not want to get his feet wet and said "No".

Tane then turned to little Kiwi bird and asked, "Kiwi, little Kiwi, will you go down to live in the darkness and dampness of the forest floor?"

"I will," replied Kiwi.

In that moment there was a great hush in the forest.

Tane spoke.

> "Kiwi, do you know that if you will do this to save my trees, you will have to lose your beautiful wings and colored feathers so that you will not be able to fly back to the roof of the forest? "
>
> "I do," replied little Kiwi.
>
> "Kiwi, do you know that you will have to grow strong, thick legs and a long hard beak, so you will be able to dig and rip up the logs and leaves to find insects on the forest floor?"
>
> "I do," replied beautiful Kiwi.
>
> "Kiwi, brave Kiwi, do you know that you will never see daytime again?"
>
> "I do," replied obedient little Kiwi.

Taking one last look at the light filtering through the leaves and the sun shining on his beautiful colored feathers, Kiwi, saying a silent goodbye, gave himself over to Tane, the great God of the Forest. Landing on the forest floor Kiwi felt the damp under his feet and his world became forever night. Brave, brave Kiwi, whose sacrifice and obedience are forever sacred in the land of the Maori forests.

Tane cursed the other birds for their selfishness.
He branded Tui with two white feathers at his throat to show what a
coward he was. He banished Pukeko to live in the marshland so his feet
would always be wet. Greatly moved by Kiwi's sacrifice, Tane proclaimed
to all who lived in the forest that for his sacrifice, Kiwi would become the
most well known of all the birds and will forever be the most loved.

Staying in the dark corner of the dog kennel assured me that all good
things come to those who sacrifice, as they had come to Kiwi. If I could
be quiet and obedient, I too might be loved even though Dad had left
and Mother was always gone in the daytime. My sister had gone away
to boarding school, which left me home alone with my brothers. We did
a lot of things together but none of them were my idea. Older brother
Jeremy did not like me very much as he was always punching me on
the arm. I tried to avoid him. Middle brother Cedric had taken my toys
apart to see if he could put them back together. Actually, all of my toys
were either broken or dead. My twin brother Rodney was not dead but
he would never play cowboys and Indians with me on the front lawn.
He didn't even own a cowboy suit, not that it mattered anyway because
more important things had to be done in church programs so there was
no time to play with anyone.

Monday night was a church program that was held at the house called
'Family Home Evening.' We spent an hour together as a family sitting
in the front room where Mother would read one Bible story and go over
the chore list for the week. Tuesday night priesthood men came to visit
as 'home teachers' to make sure Mother was doing her job to get us to
church and Thursday night ladies came from the women's church club
called Relief Society to see if Mother needed any help in the house so we
could get to church. Friday night was bath night and Saturday was slave
day to do all the chores listed on the refrigerator. The most important of
all nights was Wednesday night. This was the night where we all went
into town to the church activity hall. The boys went to boy cub scouts
and had uniforms and a flag. The girls went to a room with some shelves.
This is where we learned how to be.
Be obedient.

Be unselfish.
Be clean.
Be good.
Be perfect.

Sundays were spent all day at church where it was against the rules to play. Every Sunday morning I went to a special church class for little girls. I didn't like being with the other girls as they all talked about their new dresses or fancy shoes. My shoes had holes in them and even though I had a new cowboy suit I wasn't allowed to wear it to church. Sunday school class was boring and had no punishment kennel so I could talk a lot if I wanted to. But I never wanted to. Instead I would sit in the back row by the corner of the room where I could think a lot about Nana in heaven, Koala and the moon and brave little Kiwi in the darkness of the forest floor. I also thought a lot about my brothers.

They were being prepared to receive their power from God called the 'priesthood'. This made them special, much more special than girls. That's why all the important people at Sunday school were men. It also made them the boss of everything because God only talked to boys. God did not talk to girls but teachers in Sunday school class were sent to teach us everything we needed to know to get to heaven. I was taught about virtue, cleanliness, service, kindness and obedience.

Virtue was one part of being obedient. That meant I had to have babies for my husband, but only when he said so. It also meant that I was not to have sex contact. I really did not know what they were talking about as I had no contact with sex and nobody hugged me.

Cleanliness meant that I had to wash myself a lot. This was a major problem. I hated taking Friday night baths with my twin; he would always pee in the tub. It was also cold in there and I never knew which towel was mine. Also if I took a bath on my own I might drown and no one would come to save me. So rather than take a bath I took birdbaths like Kiwi. I would wet a small washcloth and rub a little soap on it and scrub my face, my ears (so beans would not grow), my hands, and my fingernails.

Clean fingernails were really important at home. Mother would always tell us that you could tell a person's character by how clean they keep their fingernails.

Service meant working really hard. Service was about doing things for other people instead of for you. I would rake the lawn, dry the dishes, feed my goldfish, hang my clothes up for my mother, fold the washcloths in the drawer, help vacuum the rugs, sweep the kitchen floor, clean the windows, help Cedric fix Rebecca's abandoned bike, and play with my brothers when they needed me to play with them. Middle brother Cedric always needed me to play Postman's Knock. This game we played in the closet under the stairs. Cedric would say, "Knock, knock, the postman's here." I had to say, "Do you have a parcel or a letter?" He would get to pick. If it was a parcel I had to kiss him on the mouth. If it was a letter I had to kiss him on the cheek. It was a really dumb game but I was always obedient. I would have preferred to be raking the lawn but serving the priesthood by playing the game would get me to heaven.

Kindness was more fun than service. Kindness was about being a Sunbeam. And I was. I was in the Sunbeam class in Sunday School. I had to learn a song to help me remember to be kind each day. I liked to sing the Sunbeam song,

> "...Jesus wants me for a sunbeam, to shine for him each day, in every way try to please him, at home, at school, at play. A sunbeam, a sunbeam, Jesus wants me for a sunbeam. A sunbeam, a sunbeam, I'll be a sunbeam for him..."

Occasionally we would sing the song in front of all the church people. For these performances we learned actions to go with our Sunbeam song. It was perfect.

Obedience was to do exactly what the priesthood people at church wanted me to do. This was always the same as what Mother wanted me to do. Like God, and the priesthood people, she wanted me to be perfect. Being perfect was hard.

I practiced being perfect but things didn't work out that way. Then I had to learn a scripture by heart that had no tune to it. It was, *"...As a man thinketh, so is he..."* That meant if you think something bad, you are bad and if you think you are going to actually do something bad and don't do it, it's too late, because you've already thought it. I tried to have perfect thoughts but it was hard as I had a lot of bad thoughts that nobody but me knew about. I hated Mrs. Cheverton. I hated slave day and I hated playing Postman's Knock in the closet with my brothers. These bad thoughts did not count against me in heaven because I was not eight yet. When eight came I would be baptized which would wipe away all my bad thoughts and all my bad actions. After baptism everything I did counted, and everything I thought counted on earth and in heaven. Heaven headquarters on earth was in America in a state called Utah. I knew this because by the time I was six our house was being taken over by Americans.

Sightings of my mother were scarce.
Sightings of Mormon missionaries were common.
I could never seem to avoid them. Sometimes there were two, sometimes four. Once there were eight. There was never one because they needed to be with each other to protect themselves from Satan. That's why they all slept in the same room. I could never get into the toilet in the mornings. I hid my toothbrush in case they used it by mistake. The laundry was full of hanging one-piece underwear suits called temple garments. They were always in the kitchen in the morning before I went to school ironing their white shirts. Some of them even ironed their socks. They always complained about having no frozen orange juice or stuff called margarine. They always drank water with dinner. They always wanted ice in the water. This I did not understand at all. Didn't they know that water with dinner is bad for you? Your tummy fills up with water, leaving no room for food. But water didn't seem to stop them eating big plates of food. They all rode bicycles and would often crash on our driveway. My brothers and I would watch them through the window as they raced to the house and turned into our gravel driveway.
Wipeout!
We clapped and cheered when they crashed.

They heard us.
They hated us.

They would also say prayers all the time: in the morning, in the night-time, at the table, in the living room. They also kept eating all the peanut butter.

> "Hey, stop eating all the peanut butter. You're being greedy and leaving none in the jar for us," I said when I caught Elder Hall red-handed one morning.
> "Sorry but we need peanut butter to do the Lord's work," he replied looking at me with his squinty eyes and bushy eyebrows. He was short, with short black curly hair.
> "If you eat any more peanut butter you will pop," I said.

They taught me at Sunday school that God needs me to be honest. Elder Hall was fat. His shirt buttons were pulling open.

> "Well Philippa, I will try my best to remember that," he said scooping out the very last spoonful from the jar.
> "Good, because the reason you are fat is that you eat too much peanut butter!" I said honestly.

He said nothing. He left to pray.
I said nothing. I left to walk the mile to school.
I left thinking really, really bad thoughts.

Elder Burrows killed my budgie.
Two of the birds lived in a small metal cage in the dining room; one bird sky blue, one bird sea green, each with black tips on its wings and a black hood on the top of the head. Dad had smuggled them to New Zealand on board his ship from Africa by hiding them in the air vent of his cabin. Elder Burrows told us they would be happier if they could fly freely around the house, as it was cruel to keep them in such a small cage. All he had to do was to clip their wings so they could not fly away. I thought of Kiwi and the fact that he did not have to have his wings clipped to

stay on the forest floor. It was his choice to stay. If Elder Burrows wanted to make the budgies happy all he had to do was to ask them to stay and they would. Elder Burrows also had the priesthood so the budgies would have to obey him.

He said a prayer out loud and then opened the cage.

The blue budgie took flight as soon as the cage opened. We never found it. Elder Burrows got hold of the green budgie between his hands but then he lost his grip and after a short flight around the living room, it flew up the chimney and got caught in the flue. He got it out but now the bird and the hands of Elder Burrows were covered with black soot.

Now he had to give my bird a bath.

This he did not pray about.

Rushing warm water under the tap made quick work of getting the soot off my budgie and off Elder Burrows. Back in the cage he went with another prayer to keep him safe and well. The next morning my budgie was hanging upside down with his little feet still wrapped around the perch. He was quite frozen and quite dead. He had died of a cold. Elder Burrows wrapped the stiff little body in a piece of white paper, said another prayer and buried it in the rubbish tin. I never had another budgie and I was developing a growing hatred for the Americans who had invaded our house and brought to it nothing but disruption and death.

Even when they were not in the house, things died. My goldfish was in a bowl on the hall table. It had buggy eyes and a long orange tail. Its mouth would move, but it never really said anything. It was my job to feed it every night. Sometimes I would forget so one night I gave it all the food in the little container so it would have enough food to last at least a whole week. This way if I forgot to feed it tomorrow it would have enough food until I remembered. The next morning my goldfish was floating in the bowl. It had popped. It did not know when to stop eating. That morning I took smaller portions at breakfast and I never ever wanted another goldfish.

My Grandpa Jeremy died.

He didn't have a cold like my budgie and he didn't pop like my goldfish. My Nana told me he died bringing in a load of firewood to her house. His foot came through the doorway and he just fell flat, down and dead. So, my grandmother came to live with us. When I would visit her downstairs in the basement she sat me on her knee and we played finger piano. Finger piano meant that she would lay my hands flat on her knee and tap her fingers on the back of my hands. Her fingers were strong little hammers and gently hit against my skin. She hummed the tune and hammered it out. Then I sang her my Sunbeam song with the actions. She clapped. Then I would recite the only poem I knew.

> *"When I was one I was just begun,*
> *When I was two I was nearly new,*
> *When I was three I was hardly me,*
> *When I was four I was not much more,*
> *When I was five I was just alive,*
> *But, now that I'm six, I'm as clever as clever and I think I'll stay*
> *six forever and ever!"*

Some months later an ambulance came down the driveway and backed up to the front door. They wheeled Nana into the back and took her away. I was told that she had a bad cold called 'pneumonia' and that she needed to go to the hospital to get medicine to get well. I knew what a cold could do and if this was a really bad cold, well, I just hated the thought of her being frozen like my budgie. Six days later they brought her back. Mother put her in the downstairs bedroom, which was close to the downstairs toilet, the phone and the front door. I sang my Sunbeam song to her from the bottom step of the hallway staircase.
She clapped.
I said my poem.
She clapped.
In that moment life was perfect.

One school night Nana asked mother if she could please have some fresh oysters. Nana really liked oysters, especially straight from the ocean out of the shell. Wanting to make her happy, Mother went down to the village in the middle of the night and got the local fish shop owner out of bed to sell her a dozen fresh oysters to bring home for Nana to enjoy, which she did.

Sitting up in her bed she gleefully ate the whole dozen.

The next morning I woke up to the sound of the ambulance backing down the driveway. Doors opened and they wheeled Nana once again into the back. This time she was fully covered under a white cloth.

When I got home from school, a church person told me that Nana had gone to heaven; that she had died in her sleep and that I was not allowed to go to the cemetery to see her put in the ground. They told me I was too young to understand such things. But they were wrong. I did understand such things. Like my budgie and my goldfish, she would not be back. Like my budgie and my goldfish, she was covered in white to be buried in a rubbish tin and sent to heaven.

In Sunday school I learned that dead bad people go to hell and dead good people go to heaven but in Mormon heaven there were three or four different kinds of heaven. To get to the best heaven you had to be baptized and do some other things that they did in the big temples. You had to be perfect to get into the temple. Then there was the middle kind of heaven that took middle kind of people. Then there was the lower heaven that took people who did not fit the other two heavens but were not bad enough to go to hell. Nana was not a Mormon but I knew that Nana was a good person so she was going to go to heaven. I just couldn't figure out which one. Maybe there was another heaven for good people who were really good even though they were not Mormons. Maybe God would let her into the top heaven if I told him that Nana was perfect.

I missed Nana.

No more finger piano.

No more poems.

No more singing.

No more did I want to be six.

Chapter 5

Matthew 5:44

"But I say unto you. Love your enemies, bless them that curse you, do good to them that hate you, and pray for them which despitefully use you, and persecute you."

I don't remember becoming seven. I just woke up seven. Seven was the year my brother Cedric caught himself on fire when he decided to make a campfire down on the lower lawn behind the house. Equipped with the can of motor-mower petrol from the garage his adventure in campfire basics began. Pouring petrol all over the twigs and sticks from the small shrubs that lined the fence line, Cedric failed to notice the splash of petrol now soaking into his worn leather shoes and long knee-length school socks. Crouching low over his campfire, the heavy pull of his small wooden kitchen match sent sparks across and down the side of his matchbox to explode the pool of petrol.

Whooooosh!!!!

The screams coming up the driveway alerted my mother working in the kitchen and turned my head to watch flaming, running legs headed for the back porch where my mother ran to meet him. Down to the ground he went with Mother's beating hands slapping the woolen kitchen mat against his thighs and lower legs. The commotion ended with Mother carrying Cedric to the couch and salve found inside the house. Lasting what seemed only seconds I resumed my Cowboy and Indian adventures on the front lawn with my lasso and my dog Tootie, a small black and white fox terrier. There was nothing for me to do about Cedric. I could never do anything to save him as he was always getting himself, or us, into some kind of trouble. Besides, I had a bigger problem of figuring out how I was going to lasso the letterbox.

The wooded acres down in the gully below the Morrison family house was thick with spreading oak trees, tall kauri pines, dense fern laden bush with a creek that trickled through the shade from the upper green grass paddock. Cedric, Rodney and I often played in the woods with the Slidell brothers and the two older Morrison boys. On one such occasion out of the rustling tall ferns we heard Cedric yell for help.

"Ahhhhhhhhhhhhhhhh" came his scream.

We all ran in his direction.
He ran with his arms waving all about his head.
Unlike the cartoons we had seen on the neighbor's television set, the bees were not in the shape of an arrow.

> "Get them off me!!" Cedric screamed as he ran through the surrounding hedges of prickles and thorns.
> "Run faster! They are all over your head!" yelled Adrian Slidell who was behind him in chase.
> "Get to the paddock. Get to the paddock!" shouted the Morrison boys in unison as we were in full flight through the bush.

The swarm followed us as we bolted through the thicket to the sight of both Morrison parents running full speed down the hill. As soon as we hit open field the bees disappeared as quickly as they had arrived leaving Cedric with nineteen stinging bites on his head, eyes swollen shut, and lips puffed up like balloons.

Getting rid of the Morrison parents was not as fast as getting rid of the bees. The ambulance took Cedric away and after a forever afternoon of rules and more rules and the shaking of fingers it was decreed by the old people in the room that the Gordon kids, the Morrison boys, and the Slidell brothers were officially banned from ever going down into the woods again.

Three days later we went to the woods.
Again.

We needed money.

We all knew it was harder since Dad had left because Christmas presents came from church and shoes had to last. Complaints were never voiced and holes in our shoes were hidden from Mother's glance. We knew that we had to cover the expense for sweets and we knew we needed nine pennies each to go to the Saturday afternoon picture show at the village cinema. Cedric came up with the plan to make acorn men that we would sell on the street in front of our house. At half a penny each we would have to sell eighteen each.

Each acorn man used two acorns.

Thirty-six acorns per person.

Thirty-six acorns multiplied by four Gordon's.

The only place to get one hundred and forty four acorns was in the woods.

In truth, God was probably really proud of the fact that Cedric had started a business venture to help us work hard and be fruitful. We knew this because we prayed for God to make the bees stay in their hive and for God to make the Morrison parents invisible.

God always answered our prayers.

God also made us really quiet.

God was really proud of the fact that we were helping the poor.

Cedric was really proud of the fact that we were obedient.

I was really proud of the fact that we carried a full sack of acorns up the hill. We never knew what Mother was proud of, and she never knew we were in the woods.

Acorn man production instructions:

Gather two acorns, five matchsticks and a fork.

Get one acorn with a hat on. Poke a hole in the other end. Stick a wooden matchstick up the hole. Get another acorn without a hat. Poke a hole in the top and join it to the other acorn. Poke holes in the top acorn for arms and add two matches for arms. Poke holes in the bottom acorn for legs. Get two matches with red tips for shoes and poke them in the leg holes. Line up the acorn men laying down flat on a metal tray. Put the 'For Sale' sign up, and wait for a customer. Look sad.

Three weeks of sad later, we reached the day when we walked the two miles to the village to see a picture show. It was a Saturday afternoon. There was a line at a cage on the side of the building where you gave the old lady your pennies.

> "May I have one ticket please?" I said pushing seven pennies and four halfpennies across the worn wooden counter and under the cage.
> "One ticket. Enjoy the show!" she replied with a wink and a smile pushing a small gray numbered stub toward my open hand.

As usual, Cedric led the way.

The picture house was dark and smelled like old furniture polish. Wooden seats in wide rows faced the front curtain that was red velvet with a big gold fringe at the bottom. Sitting between Rodney and Cedric my eyes focused on the red, blue and green lights that flashed up and down on the curtain. I thought about all the work we had done to sell our acorn men. I thought about the fact that we would have to sell more of them to come back.

The lights started to dim.

It was time!

The red curtains began to rise.

The lights went dark.

Everybody clapped.

The New Zealand national anthem played with a picture of Queen Elizabeth on the screen.

We all stood up to attention like we had been trained to do at school.

> "...God defend New Zeeeee- a- land..." we sung in chorus.

Done. Over. Sit.

The Queen left.

All at once the white screen exploded into words and moving pictures!

It was 'Tarzan Of The Jungle' swinging from tree to tree, swimming away from crocodiles, fighting brown people with spears, wrestling with giant hairy spiders, talking to the animals and diving over waterfalls!
We never had this kind of adventure in our woods.
We never had waterfalls in our woods.
We never had monster hairy spiders in our woods.
We only had bees. And, we never talked to them anymore.
Tarzan's jungle was much more exciting than ours although he was in more trouble than we could ever imagine.
My eyes widened. I hated spiders, especially big ones like the daddy long legs in my wardrobe. And, just as Tarzan was about to be eaten by a big monster black spider the film stopped.

> "Why did the film stop?" I whispered to Cedric. "Is it broken?"
> "Because they want you to come back next week to see what happens," he said.
> Cedric always had the right answer.
> "What do we do now?" I asked.
> "Shhhhhh, the main picture is about to begin," he replied with a snap.

'Lilly' was a movie about this girl like me who felt really alone so she went to the circus where she met a man who helped her get better. She also met all of his puppets. She made me smile. She made me cry. Clinging to the high wire pole and wanting to jump all the way to the ground, Lilly was so sad that she wanted to hurt herself because none of the adults loved her. She didn't have any real friends to save her. She didn't have anyone to tell her secrets to other than the puppets and they weren't really real so they didn't really count. I didn't have any puppets but I did have my real dog Tootle. I didn't have any circus friends but I did have my real brothers. In the darkness of the movie house and mesmerized by the flicker of a thousand frames, I wondered who was going to save me.

We never sold enough acorn men to go to another picture show. I had worked hard believing that God would surely send someone to buy them. It didn't happen. God and Mother didn't want us to see another picture show. I was thinking good thoughts to develop my character and some bad thoughts about wanting to see another picture show. Mother would not give us any money. She never gave us money.

It was God's fault that we didn't sell enough acorn men!
I was told that good things came to those who sacrifice.
The picture show was a really good thing. Maybe I hadn't sacrificed enough and God knew it. Maybe God had heard my bad thoughts so I didn't deserve to go to another picture show. Maybe he was punishing us for going back into the woods.

Mr. Spencer came to my rescue so I didn't have to have any more bad thoughts about not being able to go to see another picture show. The Spencer's lived on the other side of the empty lot and owned the only black and white television set on the street, maybe even in the village. Philip and Andrea Spencer were twins just like us but they were in the class at school ahead of us. Mr. Spencer worked fixing power poles and Mrs. Spencer stayed at home to cook and hang the washing on the line.

Every Friday at half past four in the afternoon, Mr. and Mrs. Spencer invited us over to their house to watch the small television set in the living room. Seated on the floor we got to watch either 'Rin Tin Tin' or 'Robin Hood.' Robin Hood was always doing good things for other people even though like us, he really didn't have permission to be in the woods. I bet his band of men made acorn armies. Rin Tin Tin was a cowboy dog that played Cowboys and Indians, just like me, and my dog Tootie.
'Robin Hood' was my favorite show.
'Rin Tin Tin' was my favorite show too.
But our world of television ended suddenly when Mr. Spencer was electrocuted at the top of a power pole. We never went next door again and just as suddenly as Mr. Spencer had died, Andrea, Philip, the television, and Mrs. Spencer moved away.

I did not think about picture shows after they moved.
School had started and I was in a new class.

Mrs. Lancert was my teacher. She was shorter than Mrs. Cheverton and had dark black hair, black eyebrows, and hairy arms. I had not improved very much as I still talked a lot, mainly to Rodney, in class. One day she got mean and brought me up to the front of the class. I did not see a dog kennel so I wondered what my punishment was going to be.

"Hold out your hand," she said from her desk.

I bent my elbow and held my hand out. Maybe she was going to give me something to take back to my desk.

"Hold your hand straight out in front of you with your fingers together," came the next command.

She came over to me from her desk. In her hand was a thick leather strap. My body tightened and my teeth clenched hard together. This was going to hurt. And everyone would see it hurt. I became determined that I was not going to cry. Little Toot never cried when he was punished. I stood still staring straight ahead at the back wall. Mrs. Lancert brought her arm up and over her head.

Thwap! The strap went across the center of my palm.
"Ouch," I thought inside my head as the sting reached my elbow.
Silence.

Mrs. Lancert brought her arm up and over her head.
Thwap! The strap went across the center of my palm.
I clenched my teeth and could feel my hand begin to swell.
Silence.

Mrs. Lancert stopped after the sixth slap across my red and blistered hand. The pain had numbed my arm.
The room was silent.

"Get back to your desk," she ordered.

I walked in measured steps to my hard wooden chair and quietly sat down. I glanced at Rodney. He had watery eyes. I didn't.

One week later our class went on a field trip to visit the Auckland zoo. It was an all day outing. By this time I did not like Mrs. Lancert very much at all. Even though she did not have a dog kennel, she was still very mean. I gently rubbed my hand, which was still tender from the strap the week before. School must be like church. The grown-ups make the rules and they punish you if you do not obey them. If I was going to survive school I best work harder and keep quiet.

"No talking on the bus!" Mrs. Lancert yelled.

We were instructed to look out the window at all the sights of the city. Arriving at the zoo was so exciting it was hard to keep the wonder inside my mouth. The first animal we saw was a huge elephant. It was the biggest animal I had ever seen. Holding on to the hands of my classmates and Rodney, Mrs. Lancert guided us from cage to cage. Suddenly I heard the roar of a lion! We turned the corner and there it was.

Standing in front of Mrs. Lancert, Rodney and me, was a lioness bigger than the dead one on the floor in Rodney's room. It was a beautiful creature with strong shoulders and really large paws. Her teeth were long and she had eyes that watched our every move. Her eyes met my eyes. For a moment I wondered if she knew about the dead lioness on the floor at home, or Mrs. Cheverton's dog kennel, or the fact that Mrs. Lancert had given me the strap six times. I wondered if she knew that my cage was as small as hers.

All at once the lioness turned away from us leaving her tail toward us. Mrs. Lancert took this opportunity to tell us that this lioness had come all the way from Africa. I knew this. Suddenly the lioness lifted her tail. A high-pressure stream of pee shot out of the cage.
I ducked!
Rodney ducked!
Mrs. Lancert did not duck.

The steaming hot pee hit her hair and face and washed down the front of her cardigan. She screamed an awful scream and began to gulp for air at the same time that little gaggy coughs escaped from her mouth. Spitting pee on the footpath as she ran, Mrs. Lancert bolted for the public toilets. We stayed perfectly still.

Done with her business, the lioness very slowly lowered her tail and resumed her measured pacing back and forth from edge to edge in the tiny cage. My stare followed the glow of her fierce hazel eyes.

> "I am going to be strong like you when I grow up" I said
> to myself.

I rubbed my sore hand.
The lioness must have heard my thoughts.
I smiled a very small smile.
Mrs. Lancert and I were now even.

CHAPTER 6

MATTHEW 5:6

"Blessed are they which do hunger and thirst after righteousness: for they shall be filled."

◇ ◇ ◇

The day of my bad thought removal process had come.

I was eight. My baptism was scheduled for Sunday after church. The congregation and my brothers were invited to watch by sitting in lines of grey metal folding chairs placed in neat tidy rows behind an accordion heavy green plastic room divider. Behind the divider, cold pale green tiled stairs led down to a baptismal font that was the size of a very small swimming pool. A small room to the side of the steps housed a changing room with cubbyholes to put my towel. Everything had to be white; white dress, white underwear, white socks, white towel, white walls and white thoughts.

Once changed, I started nervously down the steps. This was like taking a really big bath in your clothes. Knee deep my dress immediately began to float on the warm water. I quickly pushed as hard as I could down on either side of the floating material until water lapped over my hands and the dress stuck tight to my legs. My thoughts immediately went to the fact that it would have been easier to wear my yellow polka dot bikini that my sister had bought me to wear at the beach. But, Mother told me I had to wear white and I had to wear a big white girly dress.

Now I was wading waist high in warm water toward one of the missionaries wearing a white jacket, white tie, white shirt, white long pants, white Mormon underwear, white socks, a white teeth smile and who was wet. He faced out to the people in seats and I faced sideways and began to count the tiles.

"Sister Gordon," he said bringing my focus to his blue eyes, "Welcome. Let me show you how I need you to be today."

He placed my left hand on his left wrist. He then put my other hand in his hand so I could hold my nose when he pushed me under the water. John the Baptist must have told Jesus the same thing in the river so he wouldn't get water up his nose. Holding his right hand up like a stop sign he began to speak.

> "Having been given the Melchezidek priesthood and all the rights that it bears, I baptize you, Philippa Gordon, in the name of God the Father and his son Jesus Christ, Amen."

He brought his right hand down to my back.
He pushed with the arm I was holding.
I took a deep breath.
Down into the water I sank under the pressure of his forearm for what seemed to be forever.

I hated being ducked by my brothers in the pool and this felt exactly the same. I was worried that my dress might float up to the surface or not go under the water all the way. Bad thought removal wouldn't work if you did not go down all the way. His push reversed. I surfaced.

Wiping the water from my face I now stood waist deep in warm water wearing wet white clothes that were clinging to every part of my body. Jesus must have had the same problem with his long robes but he never talked to us about how he felt in that moment. Other than wet, I felt no different. That was to be expected I suppose given that I didn't have the Holy Ghost yet. That was to be the feeling part of it. That was the next part of thought removal.

Back in the dressing room I dried off and changed back into my usual worn out Sunday clothes. Coming once more into the room of people I was led to a chair that faced everyone. I sat with my hands in my lap. Three priesthood men in suits stood around me and gently placed all six warm dry hands over the entire top of my head. Silence. With all heads bowed in the room, three drops of special consecrated olive oil were dripped on the crown of my skull.

> "Philippa Gordon, by the power of the Melchezidek priesthood I confer upon you, the power and presence of the Holy Ghost by which you will come to know and receive great blessings from your Father in Heaven and by which you will know the truth of all things in the name of Jesus Christ, our Savior, Amen."

Like my Sunbeam song, the Holy Ghost was going to remind me to be kind and have good thoughts. Unlike my Sunbeam song, the Holy Ghost, they told me, would give me all the answers I needed. All I had to do was to ask.

Having the Holy Ghost inside me was a problem.
Now I had no privacy at all.
Now I would be in very serious trouble if I had any bad thoughts because the Holy Ghost would know them at the same time I knew them. Now I had to find a way to hide my bad thoughts or better yet, not even think them. I felt set up to fail as I was already having bad thoughts about having bad thoughts! And now there were two of us, me *and* the Holy Ghost. I could not see how this was a good thing because how could I protect the Holy Ghost as well as myself from my brothers and my thoughts?

I asked the Holy Ghost if we could arrange some times when he was not inside me. That would give him a holiday and me some privacy, especially in the bathroom. I also did not want him around when I was in the dressing room at the swimming pool, or when I got changed into my pajamas at night. I did want him around at school so I would know what to study and I did want him around after school to walk home with me. I made it clear to the Holy Ghost that we would have to negotiate any special times when he needed to ignore my thoughts. What a hassle. From this moment on I had to be really vigilant about everything.

My life would never be the same again. Today, unlike yesterday, every-thing I thought and did was going to be recorded in heaven. Everything I thought or did was going to be public information. I silently wished that this day and eight years old had never come.   .

I was surprised that Mother attended my baptism as I thought she had moved away. I still went to bed on my own and Cedric and Jeremy did most of the cooking. My older sister, Rebecca, was not often in the house. My brothers had told me that she was at boarding school. She was work-ing on passing her school certificate so she could apply to university to learn how to dig up old cities. She wanted to discover places and things and she was good with her hands. She was also a very good swimmer. This would be helpful in discovering underwater sea caves. She could swim for five miles and she was on the school diving team.

Late one night the village bus stopped by our house. Rebecca got off and walked down the driveway with her suitcase. She was dressed in her uniform. It was a turquoise blue pinafore with a belt and a turquoise blue boxy blazer with the school emblem embroidered on the top handker-chief pocket, long white knee socks and brown-laced shoes. On her head was a black beret pushed to the side of her ginger short hair. She and some Maori boys had been suspended from school for breaking into the swimming pool for a midnight swim. Rebecca never went back. Mother needed her at home to help look after us. She got a job in a florist shop down in the village and never spoke of digging up cities again.

We moved.
No one talked to me about moving.
The subject was not mentioned in Family Home Evening. Mother and the priesthood men at church had made the decision that we needed to move south to Hamilton. But Hamilton was eighty miles away and until this moment I had never heard of Hamilton.

Going to Hamilton was also a problem. I would have to leave my school and my favorite tree down at the beach. I was told to leave Tootie behind with some other people, as the house we were going to rent in Hamilton did not allow animals. Church people came to help us pack things in boxes and put everything into a large truck. Mother rode in the front with the driver. My brothers and I were packed in the back with the furniture and the beds. As we were not in boxes, I grabbed my small dog Tootie and went to hide in the darkness of the back of the van. Doors closed. The engine started with a jerk. Tootie let out an excited bark.

"Shhhhhh, keep her quiet!" Cedric yelled in a loud whisper.

I held her tight and tried to cover her up with some bedding.
The van stopped. We were not out of the driveway.
The back door swung open.
Light blinded my eyes as Mother grabbed Tootie out of my arms despite our pleading and cries for her to make an exception.

"There are no exceptions." Mother stated.

Moving to Hamilton was like going to Hell.
All that I had known to be real I had to leave by the sea.
My street, my school, my room, my dog, the view of the reef from the big window, the Morrison boys, the acorn men, the creek, my cowboy suit, the lioness pelt, a goldfish bowl, a birdcage, Nana's empty room, and little piano fingers playing on the back of my hand at the bottom of the stairs. I was told by Mother that the house in Hamilton was going to be small so I would have to share a room with somebody else.

Sitting in the back of the van and peering into the darkness of furniture shapes, I began to cry.
In the silence I remembered that going to Hamilton required sacrifice.
Going to Hamilton required that I be brave and tough like my brothers.
Mother needed me to be brave.
No exceptions.

There was no room for tears; there was only room for work and obedience.
I believed in my Sunbeam song.

I believed that Cedric would look after me.
I believed the Holy Ghost would look after us.
Then why did my heart begin to feel sore.
Sacrifice was beginning to hurt.

CHAPTER 7

MATTHEW 5:5

"Blessed are the meek: for they shall inherit the earth."

◇ ◇ ◇

My mind remembers very little about being nine. I don't remember going to church, although we must have gone every Sunday. Family Home Evening was always on Monday night but I don't remember ever going and I don't remember any missionaries in the house. I don't remember going to school, walking to school, doing homework or who my teacher was. There were no pets to remember. There were no friends to remember. I don't remember my mother in the house even though she came to dinner and Saturday slave days always happened. I don't remember if the Holy Ghost was on the inside of me or on the outside of me. There were lots of prayers but I don't remember any of them. All I remembered of being nine was the house, the fort, the knife, and the kisses.

As my world faded in a two-hour trip in the back of a furniture-filled van I began to collect my bad thoughts and my tears in order to stuff them one mile at a time into the little matchbox I kept in the corner of my heart. The van came to a stop outside a little brick house with a flat front lawn and no fences. Number nine Ascot Road was a sad looking place that sat square to the road and only had one level of house and a small letterbox by the curb. There was no driveway, no garden, no woods, no window blinds, no balconies, no big windows, and no ocean view. To the left and right of the house was another row of little orange brick houses that looked exactly the same as ours. I memorized our number, number nine, so I would not walk into the wrong house.

We unpacked.
I was assigned the bedroom in the front of the house. It had a very small window and it was opposite the toilet. It had two small single beds, one

for me, and one for my sister Rebecca. The boy room was in the back of the house. It had a bunk bed for Rodney and Cedric and a single bed in the corner for Jeremy. My mother slept alone somewhere else.

We settled in.

Two weeks later Cedric declared that we had to build a fort to protect ourselves from the neighbors at number eleven Ascot Road. The two boys that lived there would call Cedric names and throw stones at him on the way to the school so Cedric's project became to design and build, with us as slave labor, an intricate and large fort. It was to be located at the far corner of the back lawn, contain a central command area, two artillery outposts, and a secret entrance.

The command area was a circle about four feet wide and three feet deep. Two trenches were dug which went to small dugout artillery positions close to number nine property line which allowed us a good view and range to hurl our stones. These positions were the only part of the fort that did not have a roof of tin and wood that we had scavenged from somewhere I don't remember. A thick layer of dirt would hold the roof down and make it impossible for number eleven to score a direct hit.

> "Incoming!" Cedric would yell as we hit the dirt on our bellies and waited for the rumble of stones on the dirt above.
> "Battle stations!! Battle stations!!" shouted Cedric at full command volume.

We kept buckets of small stones at the end of each tunnel.
Throw and duck.
Duck and throw.
In the dirt and the dark, we would wait for our orders and another round. In Cedric's world the fort was a great success and as such he named it the *'Alamo'* after some picture show he had seen at school. He even made a flag for our underground hideout that stuck up by our secret entrance.

To this day I have no reason to think that going to war with number eleven was a good idea. The *Alamo* was a dangerous place. The roof could collapse and bury us alive at any moment. There was little air circulation and lots of bugs. In hindsight, it was clear that my brothers of number nine were the real bullies on the street. Jeremy was never the instigator of fights but would always win them. Rodney was around but I don't remember where or how often. Cedric was always around marking our territory and protecting it. Cedric was always in control of when the stones would come and when the stones would go.

Cedric was my hero, like Robin Hood. He was always doing work for everybody else and he always worked harder than anyone else. Cedric was also my guardian angel. Every week we did the dishes together, vacuumed the carpets together, dusted the shelves together, scrubbed the floors together, washed the clothes together, hung the clothes on the line together, sorted the clothes together, folded the sheets together, baked cakes together, filled the coal bin together, burned the rubbish together and cooked dinner after school together. On Saturdays, I would rake the grass into piles after Cedric had mowed the lawn. It took the rest of the morning to move the piles to a bigger stinky pile in the back yard.

My twin Rodney was not my hero and I never understood why his bones were so lazy. Rebecca disappeared from the house and I don't remember where she went. My oldest brother Jeremy was the enemy as he often punched my arm for reasons I don't remember. The only time we were in the same room together was when dinner had to be cooked.

Dinner had to be ready on the table by the time Mother came home from work. This routine was organized by Cedric who kept the chore list up to date, checked off the list for us, told us exactly what to do, and exactly when to do it. Rodney tried to do as little as possible. He would usually set the table and then disappear. Jeremy would get home from high school and routinely drag Rodney out of his room and into the kitchen. Rodney would mumble and moan a lot. Cedric had no patience for it, especially on busy dinner nights. Things had to get done and we prayed every night in family prayer that we would have the strength to do our jobs well. Our rewards would come on Sunday. Our rewards would also come in heaven.

> "Rodney, come and set the table!" Cedric yelled from the kitchen.

Rodney was listening to his science project radio. No answer.

> "Rodney, come and set the table! Now!" he yelled again.

Jeremy walked in the front door. I kept my head down and my eyes on the peeler and the big potato in my hand. The church home teachers were coming to dinner tonight. There would be seven of us. That's a lot of potatoes. I worked as fast as I could without cutting myself with the peeler. Cedric was working on the cabbage. He had taken the outside leaves off, washed it under cold water and was now slicing it into thin strips with a large wood-handled knife. He put a pot of water on the stove to boil the potatoes. He put another pot of water on the stove to boil the cabbage. Jeremy would cook the meat. Jeremy always cooked the meat.

Cedric was getting red in the face.

> "What are you yelling about?" asked Jeremy.
> "It's Rodney, he's not pulling his weight again," replied Cedric.
> "I'll see about that!" said Jeremy, stomping towards the back bedroom.

I kept peeling. I heard the commotion, the yells, the hits, and the crying. Cedric and the Holy Ghost did not like lazy people. Lazy people were tools of the devil. It was better for Rodney to be punished by Jeremy than become a tool of the devil. Rodney finally came to the kitchen to do his job. His eyes were red from crying and a new line of fresh bruises appeared on his right arm.
He got busy setting the table.
I continued peeling.

We were running late and Mother would be home very soon. Cedric was visibly anxious. He chopped the cabbage at an alarming speed. In between chops he was telling Rodney what he had missed on the table. I was peeling as fast as I could.

I felt his glare. Cedric was losing his temper.

"Philippa! Hurry up with the potatoes!" he demanded.
"I am, I am!" I snapped back.
"Don't you ever answer me back!" he screamed in his white rage as he lifted me off the stool by my collar and slammed me against the wall.
"Do you hear me, do you hear me!" he yelled.

His breath blew his shouts up my nose and inside my head.
I didn't see it coming.
I only heard it land.
His large wood handled knife slammed into the wall beside my left ear tearing into the wallboard as it sunk deep with his thrust into the wood framing. He began to pull the knife out of the wall.

The war in my head started. Keep still. Keep still. Be obedient. Be obedient. My mind told me to stay true to the lessons I had learned in Sunbeam class. Think good thoughts. My mind told me that the Holy Ghost was watching over me. Keep still. Keep still. Be obedient. Be obedient. My other mind told me that the Holy Ghost had left because I was big enough to peel the potatoes on my own without his help. My other mind also told me that Cedric would not miss my head if the knife came at me a second time. Keep still. Keep still. Be obedient. Be obedient.
No.
No!
No!!
I wrenched away from his grip, ducked under his arm and ran for my life to the bathroom - the only room in the house with a lock on the door. I heard the knife rip out of the wall. I heard his footsteps running to catch me. The sliding bathroom bolt caught the metal strap the moment before Cedric's body weight slammed against the door. I held my breath.

Silence.

Footsteps went back into the kitchen.
The knife began once again chopping on the cutting board.
Cedric was back on task with the cabbage.

As long as I could hear Cedric in the house I stayed locked and shaking on the toilet seat forever. Then I heard the front door open. Mother was finally home. I slid the deadbolt on the door open and very slowly and quietly opened the door.
All clear.

I ran to my room, closed the bedroom door behind me and slid down the darkest corner of the room to the floor to be as small as I could be in order to hide from Cedric or the Holy Ghost who might be looking for me. My heart began to hurt again.

I began searching in my head for the lesson; the lesson of the knife in the wall. I scanned recent events but could not think of anything that I had done to deserve my brother's anger. I asked the Holy Ghost to find the lesson but don't remember if he was in the room and I don't remember ever getting his answer. My head was getting sore.

My back pressed tight to the crack in the wall. All I ever did was what my brother Cedric asked me to do. Why had he put a knife in the wall beside my head? Why was he trying to hurt me? Why would he yell at me that way? Why didn't the Holy Ghost grab the knife? Why didn't they teach me about this in my Sunbeam Sunday class? I thought about lessons learned in my Sunbeam class. I thought about sacrifice again. I thought about my lessons in Sunday school.

There was only one story in Sunday school class and the Bible that had a knife in it. The prophet Abraham was told to kill his son Isaac with a knife as a test of his faith. The knife must have come as close to Isaac's nose as the cabbage knife came to me! Isaac must have been just as scared as I was. He didn't run to the bathroom. He just lay there very still. He just lay there very quietly. I began to feel bad about running to the toilet. Next time I just needed to lay very still and very quiet even if my mind told me not to. There it was! I had figured out the lesson! The knife in the wall was a test of my faith. Cedric was teaching me about faith!

He held the same priesthood from God as Abraham. There was no need for me to question him about anything, especially something as trivial as the potatoes. Cedric was also my favorite brother and I knew that like God, he loved me too. In fact, God had sent Cedric to look after me first and the Holy Ghost as second; a backup imaginary Cedric in case the real Cedric was not around. The knife in the wall was a reminder that Cedric, like Abraham, had great love and great power. Abraham had power over Isaac and Cedric had power over me.
God wanted it that way.
God made it that way.

I felt very special that God would take the time to teach me with a knife like he had taught Isaac. I felt very bad about my bad thoughts toward Cedric while I was in the toilet. My heart was getting sore again. Pulling my back away from the crack in the wall I pulled myself onto my knees by the side of my bed and I bowed my head and whispered a message to God into my pillow. The Holy Ghost would take it from there.

> *"Father in Heaven, thank you for my brother Cedric. Thank you for this house and for the food in the fridge. Thank you for sending the Holy Ghost. Thank you for all your blessings. Please forgive me for being bad. I promise I will do better. Father, please help me get better at faith. Father in Heaven, thank you for your lesson of the knife. Next time, please help me be very still and be very quiet. Thank you for the sunshine today. Thank you for my Sunbeam class and Father in Heaven, I humbly ask that I can be your Sunbeam forever. These things I pray for – "*

My prayer was interrupted by knocks on the front door. The church people had arrived and dinner had to be served. All hands on deck.

I said nothing and told no one about my faith lesson. I was being humble. I sat quietly and ate my cabbage. I hated cabbage. I piled mashed potatoes on the back of my fork to cover the flavor of the cabbage. I silently told the Holy Ghost I hated cabbage.

The Holy Ghost told me to be quiet and still.

Being quiet and still was hard which made it the weak part of my character.

The Holy Ghost told me to be quiet all the time.

Cedric told me to be quiet all the time.

Dinner went on as if nothing had happened and Cedric's face was not white any more even though he had another knife in his hand. Our eyes finally met across the table. He smiled a little smile. We were back to normal. He had forgiven me. I was thankful that he had forgiven me and I was thankful for his great lesson on faith.

Cedric taught me many lessons that year. He taught me how to tie my tie straight. He taught me how to iron my school uniform. He taught me how to cook Brussels sprouts, cabbage and beans. I hated them all. He taught me how to swallow vegetables without tasting them. He taught me how to shoot his hunting bow and arrow. He taught me how to make a sling shot out of a coat hanger and a rubber band. Cedric had faith in me to be a good student. I told him I was a good pupil because I had earned all my obedience badges in my Sunbeam class.

Not long after the lesson of the knife, Cedric asked me to meet him in his bedroom. As usual, Rodney, Jeremy and Mother were nowhere to be seen and Rebecca had gone somewhere I don't remember. I walked into the room and immediately saw that Cedric had made a nice, cozy, little fort with the sheet from the top bunk. This fort was much better than the *Alamo* as it required no secret password and had no bugs. I climbed in.

He told me to lie down beside him. I did.

Keep still. Keep still.

Be obedient.

Be obedient.

"I am going to teach you to kiss better than you do," he announced. "This will make you better at playing Postman's Knock and it will prepare you to serve the Priesthood."

This was going to be another lesson.

He kissed me. On the lips. Lay still. Be obedient. He told me to make my lips less stiff. I did. Lay still. Be obedient. He kissed me again but longer than before. I did. Lay still. Be obedient.
The Holy Ghost told me to be quiet and be still. I remembered the lesson of the knife.
Lay still.
Be obedient.

Some were short kisses some were long kisses. Some were so long that I had to hold my breath. He told me I was doing really well. I was being a good obedient Sunbeam. He told me that boys like girls to kiss with their mouth open. I tried my best and followed his instructions but his kisses got so wet and mushy, I had to wipe his wetness off my chin. Lay still. Be obedient.
He stopped.
Lay still.
Be obedient.

He climbed out of the bunk.

"You need to practice every week to become perfect," he said on the way out the door.

Lay still.
Be obedient.
Lesson over.

CHAPTER 8

MATTHEW 5:3

"Blessed are the poor in spirit: for theirs is the kingdom of heaven"

◇ ◇ ◇

We moved. Again.

The weathered wooden house sat back from the road and was surrounded by thick trees and straggly messy bushes. Dust covered windows looked out to a long grassy driveway which met a gravel road lined by a deep drainage ditch bordered by wild prickles and blackberry bushes, steel ladders and large cement pipes. Beyond the ditch was a green grassy paddock fenced by barbed wire that held no sheep and no cows. The new house on Dayton Street was much smaller than our last one on Ascot Road. It also had no fort, no bricks, no neighbors, no television and a fireplace that didn't work! It also had no locks on any doors including the bathroom. The only place with locks on the doors was the old 1937 Morris Minor car that sat in the driveway.

At Dayton Street Rebecca had appeared again. She lived on the closed-in front porch, which must have been really cold in the damp days of winter. All my brothers lived in one room inside the house and I had to share the other inside bedroom with my mother. Sharing a room with my mother was hard, especially at night. When she came to bed she would only have on her special Mormon underwear called 'temple garments' to keep her safe. I knew this as I remembered the missionaries by the sea had the same underwear hanging in the bathroom. I thought it odd that she needed double protection because I thought the Holy Ghost was meant to keep us safe. Maybe like me, she had an arrangement with the Holy Ghost for him not to be inside her or in her bed at night. Facing the wall and under my covers I did my best to be asleep but I would hear her knees hit the floor and her whisper prayers. Whisper prayers went on for a really long time. She would then get into her bed and immediately start crying under her eiderdown. I wondered why she was so sad. I wondered how to fix her but she wouldn't talk to me. She only talked to God.

It was not until my teens that my mother informed us that my father had refused to pay child support or alimony for fear the money would be paid in tithing to the Mormon Church. I was told that in order to get out from under his obligations he had even asserted that Rodney and I were not his children and as such he did not have any financial responsibility for our upkeep. This news was hard to bear and would keep my curiosity of him confined to reading old letters and legal documents. His denial of my existence betrayed the fact that my jaw looked like his, my chin dimple looked like his and my determination to shed the shackles of the Mormon Church was just like his. As a consequence of my father's inability to be accountable to his children, my mother worked full time to keep food on the table and we got used to hand-me-downs, porridge and hot water bottles to keep us warm in the winter.

Under British rule, the New Zealand courts required Mother to wait seven years for a divorce. Separated, but not officially divorced, Mother went to a Barrister to force payment of child support. Mother pursued the child support issue through the courts to no avail. My father left New Zealand to live in Australia and far away from the legal jurisdiction of barristers and solicitors and phone calls from a desperate mother of five children. Hence, it was there in Perth, Australia until his death, that my father continued his love affair with the sea as the Captain of a sixty thousand ton oil tanker that he sailed from Australia to Hong Kong and up the coast of China.

Back at Dayton Street, Rebecca had somehow kept in contact with our father. She had met him for lunch several times in Auckland before he left for Australia. She also had his current address and telephone number in Australia. Mother and her Barrister did not. One Saturday a blue airmail letter with an Australian stamp arrived. Only Mother was allowed to collect the letters from the letterbox.

Flipping through the bills her eyes landed on the letter to Rebecca from 'Captain Gordon'. Batten down the hatches. Letter in hand Mother marched to confront Rebecca.

Incoming! A screaming match ensued.

Rebecca accused Mother of forcing Dad to leave.

Mother screamed and cried.

Rebecca screamed and yelled and said bad words.

Rebecca demanded the letter. Mother refused to give it to her.

Rebecca threw an umbrella through the porch window in anger. Glass went everywhere. She chased Mother around the house and finally snatched the letter out of my mother's hand. It was duck and cover time all over again.

Fighting began to make my hands shake and my stomach hurt.

I learned that in order to have any peace at home there had to be absolutely no reference to or no writing about, no contact with or no mention of and no inside or outside thoughts of my father. Any shadow of him had to stay in my matchbox. Forever.

Rebecca moved out. She was nineteen and pregnant.

If she had gone to her Sunbeam lessons this would not have happened. Her boyfriend, Ron Curry, was a non-Mormon, a smoker, a Coke drinker, and a drunk. Despite Mother's disapproval that Ron Curry was not a Mormon, she demanded they marry. No exceptions.

I learned much later that after two children, three moves and countless fights, Rebecca left Ron Curry. In his drunken rages he had broken her nose, her jaw, her left rib, and her right arm. Her eyes and lips were scarred from three years of cuts and bruises. She kept her daughter Briana and gave her son, Ron Junior, away to someone else. At twenty-one her life became a journey of attraction to, and constant struggle with, abusive husbands and the desperate and driving need for the love of her father.

We moved. Again.

Dayton Street was too much money for rent so we moved into a smaller two bedroom flat in a building with four other families. We bought another bunk bed. The boys were in one room, the girls in the other. The Holy Ghost moved with us but the flat was so small I never really knew in which room he lived. I had turned eleven and Cedric was now fourteen. There was no room to set up a fort for kissing lessons so for a little while Cedric cancelled them. This made me really happy.

Church members brought food to our house in paper bags. We ate porridge, potatoes and meat. Sometimes the meat was not very good. One day little white worms came out of me when I went to the toilet. In Sunday school I had learned that the people in America who murdered the modern day Prophet Joseph Smith died horrible deaths by being eaten from the inside by worms. Bad things happen to bad people. God punishes bad people and bad thoughts.

My confusion was that I thought I was a good person.
I was very active in all the church programs and I had not missed one day of Sunday school for as long as I could remember. For weeks the worms kept coming. When I got a nose tickle or an eye twitch I knew they were eating my face from under my skin. Like the men who killed the Prophet, I was being eaten from the inside out. I felt dirty on the inside. The Holy Ghost moved out of my head. I was alone.

But good things happen to those who sacrifice.
After four weeks of worms, Mother brought home some medicine. She called me to the kitchen. She called all of us to the kitchen. Filling little plastic cups, she handed medicine to my brothers and also poured some for herself and for me. That's when I knew that everyone in the family had worms! We all drank our medicine. It tasted worse than cabbage. Cedric asked Mother where the worms came from.

> "The meat we were given was not cooked well. When that happens, worms can come inside your tummy with the meat," she explained.

From that moment I lived in fear of meat and worms.
Whenever my nose itched I thought the worms were back.
No one ever told me they couldn't come back.
No one ever told me they were ever really gone.

We moved. Again.

George Gailbraith, my father's stepfather, had died in London and left Mother a large sum of English money. Mother said the money was a reward from God for paying her tithing to the church. She told us the story of the widow's mite from the Bible. God had rewarded the widow and my mother for giving their last pennies to the church.

Good things come to those who sacrifice.

We all celebrated with lots of thank you prayers to our Father in Heaven. We could now buy a house and a car of our own. We could also buy new school uniforms for Cedric, Rodney and me. Cedric was at high school and had grown out of Jeremy's hand-me-downs. Rodney and I needed new uniforms to attend Peachgrove Intermediate School. I really needed new shoes as my only pair would let water in when it rained. We could also buy new Sunday clothes for going to church.

The new house on Taranui Street was a very posh house close to the Waikato River that ran through the center of town. Cedric and Rodney had a room of their own in the basement. Jeremy had his own room. Mother and I still shared a room. It had two windows. One of the windows was very high and looked over the front porch. There were two bathrooms, a tub and a separate shower room in the washhouse where the washing machine lived. The kitchen was very big and the dining room was next to the kitchen and looked over the back yard. The yard had three levels, a high back yard with long grass and a garden, a middle back yard where the washing line was and a lower front yard that led to the basement boys' room and a huge flat front lawn. It used to be a croquet field. The living room was huge. We had a new black and white television set in one corner, and new furniture in the middle by the fireplace. The fireplace worked. The front doors were all glass with two large etchings in the center of each door panel.

The door etchings were the McKay clan family crest from Scotland. Mother said that when she saw them she knew the Holy Ghost was telling her that this was the house to buy. The Holy Ghost was not a member of the McKay clan, but the Gordon clan was related to the McKay clan.

Mother had been taking classes at church to learn how to do our family tree, so these bits of information would come to us over the dinner table. I learned that my mother's middle name, Stanton, came from the fact that she was related to George Stanton, who invented the steam engine. My mother's maiden name of Ray was the same name as General Ray. General Ray was the English general who ordered the slaughter at the Battle of Culloden. The Battle of Culloden was the final bloody and cruel defeat of Bonnie Prince Charles of Scotland. My mother thought it interesting that while her relative General Ray was riding into Culloden, my father's clan was running out the back on their way to a life of exile in Ireland. My mind went back to our old house by the sea, the shoe, the arguments, the rain, the leaving, and the hurt. Some things never change.

My relationship with Cedric had not changed.
We were still in charge of all the jobs around the house. There were more outside jobs that needed to be done at the new house. The upper yard had to be chopped with a scythe. This was my job. The middle and lower yard had to be mowed by a push hand mower and raked. The back retaining wall had to be cemented from time to time, and the rubbish bin area had to be cleaned weekly of maggots. This was my job. The sixty-foot gravel driveway had to be raked so the stones would not bunch up on the side and the rose garden had to be weeded. The car had to be washed, waxed and vacuumed. The house roof was tin and had to be painted. Cedric and I worked on this job while Rodney listened to his new Santana record. Jeremy never did anything around the new house as he was always out with his older friends.

With the move we became new members of a different Ward. There were about two hundred people in our congregation and there were four separate congregations in Hamilton. There were a lot of Mormons in Hamilton because the Utah church Mormons had set up a Mormon high school on the outside of town. Members of our church helped us move to our new house and the women from the woman's club of the church called 'Relief Society' came over and helped us clean. They also brought food over for dinner. Mormon missionaries helped stack firewood for the fireplace and a free delivery of coal arrived in a truck from somewhere to fill the large winter coal bin that sat in the garage. Visiting Home Teachers from the men's priesthood class came to visit us every week. Two ladies from Relief Society visited once every two weeks. Mormons were everywhere and the Holy Ghost must have been really busy reminding everyone to have good thoughts.

Mother was very busy in her Relief Society job and I was very busy in my church Primary class that met every Tuesday afternoon after school. My brothers were also very busy in their priesthood jobs that took a lot of time at night visiting other people in the Ward to give special blessings, especially every time they were sick. My brothers would carry little bottles of olive oil that they said was special oil for rubbing on people's heads. The missionaries had put some olive oil on my head when I got the blessing for the Holy Ghost to live with me. I had washed it off once I had made arrangement with the Holy Ghost not to be on the top of my head.

As the church building was only ten minutes from our new house, we often walked to church by going up the hill to the corner dairy shop, turning left and walking across the railway lines, turning another left to go down the hill to our church which sat on the right side of the road. After my first month at church, the boss of our church, Bishop Morrison had me come to his office for my "eleven-year old chat". His office looked like the Principals office at school with lots of books, shelves and paper. I began to scan the room for the drawer that had the strap in it.

"Hello Sister Gordon, come in. How are you today?" he asked.
"All right," I said.

He sat me down in a metal folding chair in front of his really big wooden desk.
He then went and sat behind his desk in a really big black padded chair.

"Is there anything you would like to share with me today?" he asked.
"No," I said.

This already felt like being in Mrs. Lancert's office so I wondered what he really wanted. He was the one that asked to see me so I wasn't sure why he was asking me if I had anything to share with him. There was a big silence in the room and then he spoke up.

> "Well, Sister Gordon, today I want to share with you some very important messages. Your Sunday school teacher tells me you are doing very well in class and she is very happy to have you there. Your Primary teachers tell me you like to sing and draw pictures. God has given you many talents and we are very happy to have you in our Ward. Are you enjoying the gospel?" he asked.
> "Yes," I said.

My Sunday school teacher was talking about me to the Bishop. Uh oh!

> "That's great. The Lord wants you to know today that he has sent me here as Bishop to be your Judge in Israel. Do you know what that means?" he asked.
> "No," I replied.
> "What that means is that I am the representative of Jesus Christ on this earth. My responsibility is to make sure that you obey the commandments of the Lord. Do you know what the commandments of the Lord are?"
> "Yes," I said.
> "Very good. Do you know the thirteen articles of faith as revealed to our Prophet Joseph Smith?" he asked.
> "Yes, I learned them in my Sunbeam class," I said.
> "Very good! Are you obedient to the teachings of Christ?" he asked.
> "Yes," I said.

I took the sacrament every week so everyone knew I was being good. The sacrament was a contract with God to be good. God was not to be mocked. 'Mocking God' was a Bible word for being disobedient.

"Good. Very good! Now Sister Gordon, as a young girl in the gospel, it is important for you to live a chaste and virtuous life. Do you know what that means?" he asked.

"Yes, I learned about it Sunbeam class." I said.

"That's great, I'm glad to hear that. Do you live a chaste and virtuous life? Do you have any immoral thoughts?" he asked.

"No," I said.

"Good, very good. Do you masturbate or touch your breasts?" he asked.

"No," I said.

"Good, very good. As you know that would be a sin before the Lord. As his judge in Israel and as your Bishop, I want you to know that if you have any thoughts in this area, my door is always open. I have two daughters of my own. Have you met them yet?" he asked.

"No," I replied.

"Well, I'm sure you will soon. Now, are you living by the principles of the Word of Wisdom Sister Gordon?" he asked.

"Yes," I said.

"Excellent. It's so great to have you in our Ward. I look forward to getting to know you more. We will be meeting together every month, so if you ever have any questions about living the gospel, know that I am here to help you. Do you say your personal prayers every morning and every night?" he asked.

"Yes," I said.

"Great. Well it's so good to meet with you Sister Gordon. I look forward to seeing you in church next Sunday. I'm sure you are looking forward to it as well. Do you look forward to coming to church?"

"Yes," I said.

"Good. On your way out you can send the next person in. Thank you for coming today Sister Gordon."

"Thank you, Bishop Morrison," I replied.

I walked out of his office, gave the nod to the next girl in the hall and went home. Once home, I changed out of my church clothes while thinking about whether my answers to the Bishop's list of questions were right. I wanted to be sure so that I had no room in my head for any bad thoughts. I wanted to be sure that I was sure. I wanted to be sure that the Holy Ghost was sure that I was sure as well. I wanted to be sure that the matchbox in my heart was safe. Undressing one button at a time I silently reviewed his list.

His question: Are you enjoying the gospel?
My thought: I was having fun in Primary class and I enjoyed working hard and getting all my Sunbeam badges. I enjoyed my Sunday school class but not as much as my Sunbeam class.

His question: Do you know what the commandments of the Lord are?
My thought: I had learned by heart the commandments that God gave to Moses on his mountain in Persia and I was really good at finding scriptures in the New Testament part of the Bible. I also had learned by heart commandments from the Book of Mormon. The Book of Mormon was the commandments that God gave Joseph Smith on his mountain in Palmyra, New York. I had also learned by heart the commandments from the Doctrine and Covenants and the Pearl of Great Price. The Doctrine and Covenants and the Pearl book were the books of commandments God gave Joseph Smith and his friends in Missouri and on the way to Utah.

His question: Do you know the thirteen *Articles of Faith* as revealed to our Prophet Joseph Smith?
My thought: I had learned the thirteen sentences God gave to an American prophet in the church building in Utah. Every one of them began with "We believe…" and they were written on the back of the little cards the missionaries handed out at church. I had a stack of cards assigned to give to strangers if ever they asked me about what Mormons believed. To memorize them was also a requirement for my *Articles of Faith* Sunbeam Badge on my Sunbeam sash. I had earned all my badges.

His question: Are you obedient to the teachings of Christ?

My thought: I was as obedient as I knew how to be, even at school. I had not gotten the strap once in Hamilton. I was obedient to the priesthood, which meant that I had to do everything my brothers told me to do. My thoughts and actions were ruled by obedience.

His question: Do you live a chaste and virtuous life? Do you have any immoral thoughts?
My thought: I was virtuous because I had no sex contact or a husband. Cedric also chased me down the hallway so that was covered. I had no immoral thoughts. Actually, I had no idea what 'immoral' really was. The way Bishop Morrison said the word it sounded bad, like bad thoughts. I had really been working hard at not having bad thoughts since the Holy Ghost was around all the time, except when I had worms.

His question: Do you masturbate or touch your breasts?
My thought: I did not know what a 'masturbate' was and I did not touch my breasts. I had no idea why anyone would even want to do that but the thought that Bishop Morrison cared about my breasts did not feel very good. I wondered why he just didn't talk to the Holy Ghost who knew everything anyway.

His question: Are you living by the principles of the Word of Wisdom?
My thought: Living the Word of Wisdom was easy. I did not smoke, drink tea, drink coffee, drink Coca-Cola, drink beer or vodka and I did not eat too much meat because it gave you a fat heart and worms. I knew that my body was a temple of God because the Prophet Joseph Smith said so. I had no tattoos to defile my body and I wore clothes that covered my arms, waist, and knees to be modest. And, I had already earned my Word of Wisdom badge.

His question: Do you say your personal prayers every morning and every night?
My thought: I said a little white lie to my Bishop about saying my prayers. I said my prayers, most of the time, so technically it wasn't really a lie. It was more on the 'yes' side than the 'no' side. Saying my prayers was hard because Mother was still in my room and the Holy Ghost was always

listening. I tried really hard to talk in private to God but I never knew if he was listening and he never talked back. He was probably really busy answering all of Mother's whisper prayers.

His last question: Do you look forward to coming to church?
My final thought: I had a bad thought about looking forward to going to church. There was no sleep-in day in our house and even though Sunday was God's declared day of rest, it became the busiest day of the week for me. I needed to try harder to looking forward to going to church. It just was so hard to get up so early on Sunday mornings, especially after Slave Day on Saturday.

Saturday Slave Day never changed. The usual list was up on the wall. Dusting, cleaning, vacuuming, washing dishes, burning the rubbish, cleaning the oven, cleaning the fridge, cleaning our rooms, washing the windows, emptying the fireplace ashes.
Cleanliness was next to Godliness. I knew this.
I was learning about it again in my Sunbeam class as I prepared to get my Cleanliness badge for my sash. We also had to go over it again to be prepared to enter the young adult program. That would happen when I turned twelve.

There were some other things I had to learn in Primary in order to graduate to the 'Young Adult' class in church. One of the requirements for graduation to that program was to learn how to crochet with two little needles and some wool. We had to make little round place mats for our glasses to sit on at the dining table.
This project was a waste of my time. I had the tin roof of the house to finish painting.

> "Teacher, I have other projects to do that are more impor-
> tant that crocheting. Besides, we have a tablecloth and we
> don't need any little round things for under our glasses."
> I stated.
> "Rules are rules, no exceptions," she replied.

I knew this.

> "God wants you to become a skilled homemaker for your
> eternal husband," she added.

I knew this too.

> "Sister Gordon, you also have to do this project or you will
> not graduate from Primary class to the Young Adults."

End of subject.

The fact of the matter was that I did not want to have to ask my mother for money to buy the needles or the wool. I did not get any pocket money to spend so I found it hard to justify the expense to learn something that was so useless. I only got money for school lunch. I also resented my Primary teacher threatening me if I did not complete the task. I had seen these tactics before when Rodney was threatened at school by our teacher, Mr. Powell.

Mr. Powell was trying to withhold Rodney's daily milk ration of one half pint of milk a day for the rest of the week because Rodney had been a smarty-pants. Mr. Powell had no right to punish him this way as our milk ration was ours to have from the New Zealand government.
It was our right to have our ration of milk!
The Holy Ghost and I argued his case.
I told Mr. Powell that Rodney's punishment was unfair.
He would hear none of it.

> "If you don't give my brother his rightful half pint of
> milk, I am going to sue you!" I said pointing my finger at
> him in a stern and threatening way.

I had seen my sister do this to Mother.
Mr. Powell was speechless.
It had worked.

I knew it, the Holy Ghost knew it, Rodney knew it, and now the teacher knew it.

End of subject.

The crochet subject had not ended.

Despite the teacher's threats I refused to learn how to crochet. The problem was I could not tell if it was God talking to me, via my teacher, about learning how to crochet or if it was only my Primary teacher making the rules. She did not have the priesthood or spiritual authority over me. She did, however, like to crochet. All her handbags were crocheted. They were ugly.

Bad thought.

My imagination pictured her living in a house where everything was crocheted.

Another bad thought.

I needed to let the issue settle for a while. I would try to avoid the crochet project and be as meek as I could be.

Blessed are the meek for they shall inherit the earth.

Good things come to those who sacrifice.

But learning to crochet couldn't be part of that equation.

Besides, crochet lessons were the last thing I needed to think about as I had other equations to worry about at home.

At four o'clock one Saturday afternoon, Cedric took me to my room to talk to him. Rodney was in the basement listening to his records. Jeremy was out and Mother was at a Relief Society meeting at church. I went in and sat on the edge of my bed. He sat opposite me on the edge of Mother's bed.

> "I was talking to Larry the other day. He told me he would like to go out with you."
> "Larry Dalton! Really!" I exclaimed.

Larry Dalton was sixteen, blonde, and a priest at church. His family was from England. He and Cedric were best friends.

"What do I have to do to get to go out with him?" I asked.

"Well, you need to know what to do with a boy when you go out," he stated.

"Will you teach me?" I asked humbly.

"Yeah, I'll tell Larry that he should go out with you in a few weeks. Maybe we can all go to the Saturday night stock car races together. You and Larry can sit on the embankment and David and I will sit on the seats."

"That's a great idea. When do you want to teach me?" I asked.

"We should start today I think, before Mother comes home from her church meeting. It won't take very long to get started and we can have more lessons at the same time next week. How about we get cleaned up and meet back here in half an hour," he said.

He did not wait for a reply. We both got to it. He went to the washhouse and took a shower. I went to the bathtub and ran my usual shallow bath. I hated baths. I never felt clean sitting in a tub of dirty water. I washed myself all over with a flannel while thinking of the kissing lessons at Asquith Road. The fact that he was willing to set me up with Larry Dalton was special. Larry was admired by so many of the Sunbeam girls. He did not have a girlfriend. Neither did David Johnson.

David Johnson was the son of Bishop Johnson of the Hamilton First Ward. He and Cedric were the same age, fifteen. David had dark hair and freckles and was shorter than Larry. He was training to be a mechanic in high school and would often come to the house to fix cars with Cedric. Going to the stock car races was one of their favorite Saturday night activities. All of Cedric's friends took girls to the stock car races. I had never been to them before so the thought of going was very exciting. I jumped out of the tub, dried off, changed into my only pair of little white flower and pale blue pajamas and headed back to my bedroom.

Cedric was already under the eiderdown on my bed. I jumped in on the other side by the wall. It was cozy there. He adjusted the pillow for a better kissing angle. We reviewed all the kissing lessons he had taught me at Ascot Road. I was still a good kisser and he was still a good teacher. The next lesson was about how and where to touch and hug a boy. As it was going to be complicated, Cedric suggested that he just show me what to do and then I could practice on him. That sounded like the best idea to me, too.

Cedric and I were always in agreement. He slowly unbuttoned my pajama top from the top down. He then put his left arm under my neck. His right hand came and rested on the top of my chest. His hand slowly moved around in little circles. It was warm on my skin.

Tiny circles around my chest.

Tiny circles around my left small breast.

Tiny circles around my right small breast.

Tiny circles around my belly button.

Tiny circles around my lower stomach.

His hand was under my pajama pants.

Other than toilet paper and worms, nothing had ever touched me there before.

His kisses were getting too long.

I came up for air.

He rolled on top of me.

I felt his chest on my skin.

I felt his underwear touching my private parts.

His skin was getting slippery.

I felt his mouth on my left breast.

His tongue was moving in circles.

This time he came up for air.

He had heard car tires on the gravel driveway.

Mother was home.

Stones were pelting my matchbox.

It was duck and cover all over again.

And I knew.

I knew.

I knew the lessons would be continued the following week.

I knew there would be no Sunbeam badge for the Holy Ghost.

I knew there would be no Sunbeam badge for me.
The only place left for my Sunbeams would be in my matchbox.

My world went into slow motion as I placed my only pair of white flower blue pajamas in my drawer. I don't remember what I grabbed or how I dressed. I remember that by the time Mother walked in the front door, Cedric and I sat fully dressed on the couch in the living room watching 'Lost in Space' on the new black and white television.

"Warning, warning Will Robinson!" said the robot.

Warning, warning.

CHAPTER 9

JOHN 14:15

"If ye love me, keep my commandments."

◇ ◇ ◇

Peachgrove Intermediate School was a one-mile walk from the new house. If I cut through the fields of the Hamilton boy's high school I could walk to Peachgrove in about twenty minutes. There I would have to finish Form One and Form Two. My twin brother Rodney also went to the same school but for the first time they finally separated us into different classrooms. We also had to get a new uniform; a navy blue tunic with a belt, a white shirt, maroon tie, white socks and sandals and a white panama hat with a maroon headband. The boys wore shorty short gray pants, a white shirt, a maroon tie and a gray pullover with a maroon stripe around the collar.

My Form One teacher, Miss Makin, was not like any teacher I had before. She was really nice. She also took a lot of time with me to go over subjects that were hard. I would get to school as early as I could in the mornings for Miss Makin to assign me to keep the fire in the wood stove burning so the room would warm up. During lunchtime I would play with my friend Rowhena Johnson. She was an inactive Mormon because her parents did not go to church anymore. During afternoon break I would try to spot Rodney on the playing field. Usually I would find him sitting on a bench close to his classroom. He didn't like sports. We would arrange where to meet after school to walk home together. When Rodney did not want to walk home with me, I went to town with my classmate Manu Thompson. We would meet his father at his work and they would drop me off on their way home.

It was Slave Day again. Work got done. My boy lesson got done earlier than last week as Cedric had arranged with David Johnson and Larry Dalton to take us to the stock cars. David would be here at half past seven to collect us in his car. I changed into a pair of shorts and a short-sleeved blouse with four buttons up the front. I did not need to wear a bra because my bosoms were not big enough to wear one yet. David and Larry arrived. Cedric and I jumped in the back of the car and we backed out of the driveway. This was so exciting!

The small, round, stock-car track was surrounded by high chain-link fences. In the center of the track was a grassy area where an ambulance and a fire engine were parked. Clearly, these races could get dangerous. Beyond the fence was the spectator seating area. You could either sit on wooden seats close to the track or you could sit in the long grass and ledges of the embankment. The only lights in the place were for the track and the wooden bench area. David pulled a torch out of his pocket and shined it on the dirt path.

"Right, we'll meet you at the gate later on aye," he said.

Cedric nodded and went to the seats with Larry close behind. I turned to follow.

"Hey Pip, you're with me. Come on and stay close, it's pretty dark over here," announced David.

I was confused.
I was meant to be with Larry, not David.
Cedric and Larry were half way down the hill to the seats.
David tugged on my sleeve and pulled me in his direction.
I would have to sort out my confusion later with Cedric.

Carrying a dark green woolen blanket over his shoulder with his torch in his right hand, David kept hold of my sleeve in his left hand. We followed a worn dirt path to the other side of the embankment. David was taking his time to look for a good place to see the races. Tall grass surrounded a little hill that sheltered a small cave-like notch in the side of the embankment. It was a perfect spot. He spread the blanket out and put the torch on the blanket so I could see where to sit. He was being very gentlemanly.

Sitting down beside me his arm went immediately around the back of my shoulders.

> "Are ya warm enough aye?" he asked.
> "Yes thank you," I lied.

Actually I was a bit chilly in my shorts but I didn't want him to think I was a sissy. I sat with my knees up to my chin and my hands around my legs. His arm was still draped on my shoulder.

The first race was about to begin. A man on the side waved a green flag. There was a deafening roar of engines as the cars came flying around the first bend. David and I could not hear each other so there was no need to try to talk to each other during a race. Ten laps and a lot of flying dirt, the five cars crossed the finish line. You could smell the exhaust fumes and the beer up the embankment. People somewhere behind us were throwing beer bottles in the grass and smoking Rothman cigarettes. They were clearly not obeying the Word of Wisdom. I could hear them, I could smell them, but I could not see them at all. I could barely see David.

Hunkered down in the grass against the hill, David sensed that I was getting cold so he threw one half of the blanket over my legs.

> "So what do you do at church?" I asked.
> "I'm a priest in the priesthood. I mainly serve the sacrament on Sundays and do my home teaching rounds," he replied.

Silence.

> "So Cedric told me that you're a really great kisser," he said, snuggling closer into me. I blushed.
> "I really wanna kiss ya Pip. Whadaya think aye?" he said coming closer to my face.

Silence.

I immediately thought of all the time Cedric had given me in lessons. David was not Larry. David was David. He was also a good friend of Cedric's. Good things come to those who sacrifice. I let him kiss me on the cheek.

Like Cedric, his upper lip was a little fuzzy so it tickled a bit. I giggled.

> "Whadarya laughing at aye?" he said in a joking tone.
> "Your fuzzy lip tickles," I replied.
> "Yeah, sorry about that. Let's give it another go aye and I promise it won't tickle."

He bent down and kissed me on the lips. I kissed him back just like Cedric had taught me.

David was more interested in me than the stock cars. By the third race he had wrapped us both up in the green blanket. It was warm in our little cave and his kisses had become soft and wet. By the fifth race he had unbuttoned my blouse and made circles on my chest. His body was tight to mine. I unbuttoned his shirt like Cedric had taught me.

I lost track of the race number we were up to. His right hand went down under my shorts. People up the hill were yelling and clapping. The noise of the engines became really loud. His mouth and tongue made a sucking sound on my mouth. His left hand was squeezing my breast. Pushing my leg wide all at once he was inside me. I knew I had been taught well by Cedric, but this was new. Cedric had not taught me this part.

Be quiet and still.

David has the priesthood so you are in good hands. I could feel the slight breeze rustling the tall grass. Looking far into the night sky my eyes rested on the four stars of the *Southern Cross*.

There was no Moon to pull me out to sea. There was only the weight of him on top of me.

The engines roared and my world went quiet.

The lights of the stadium faded as we drove away. I was mute in the back seat with Cedric. Once home he asked me how it was.

> "Fine," I mumbled.
> "Yeah, well, sorry about the mix up but Larry didn't want to go out with you and David did, so I knew it would be good with you," he replied on his way out the back door to the basement.

I turned to speak to him but realized he was already out the door. I went to my room. Mother was awake and reading her scriptures.

> "Did you have a good time Philippa?" she asked without looking up.
> "Yes," I said.
> "Good." She replied. "Don't forget to wash your face and behind your ears before you come to bed," she added.

I did so, more than once. I came to bed clean on the outside. The inside was another matter.

My monthly interview with the Bishop was scheduled for the next day after church. Same time, same metal chair. Bishop Morrison welcomed me and started his usual list of questions.

> "Sister Gordon, do you believe in God the Father and his son Jesus Christ?"
> "Yes," I said.
> "Do you believe in the Holy Ghost and his power to speak to his disciples?"
> "Yes," I said.
> "Are you keeping the Word of Wisdom?"
> "Yes," I said.
> "As a daughter in Israel, do you keep a chaste and virtuous life?"

Silence.

Bishop Morrison could see my hesitation with the question. I was thinking about the thought of having a husband and having babies. Having
babies had got to hurt. Bishop Morrison was suddenly beside me in his
rolling chair. He picked up my hands in his. I was waiting for him to kiss
me. It didn't happen.

> "Sister Gordon, do you know what that means when I say
> a chaste and virtuous life?"

I reiterated the meaning of virtue as I learned it from Sunbeam class. The
Bishop was very pleased and he squeezed my hand in appreciation. I
did not want to get Cedric into trouble about me being chased down the
hallway with the knife.

I stalled.

> "Bishop Morrison, could you please explain 'chaste' some
> more so I can be sure of my answer?"
> "Sure. I'll tell you exactly what I tell my own daughters.
> Being chaste means that you have precious gifts in store
> for your chosen high priest and husband, and your gifts
> are so precious to God that he wants you to look after
> them. Sister Gordon, your gifts are the gifts of life. Within
> you is the power to create children with your eternal hus-
> band. Therefore, you need to be vigilant in keeping pure,
> modest and spotless before your father in Heaven and
> the Holy Ghost. Do you understand what I am saying?"
> "Yes," I said. His answer was not what I had expected.
> Cedric was in the clear.
> "Sister Gordon, are you living a chaste and virtuous life?"
> "Yes," I said.
> "Good. Are you in any way touching your own body in
> ways that are unclean like masturbation?"

There was that word again. I had to know what he was talking about.

"Bishop Morrison, can you please tell me what a masturbation is so I can answer your question?" I asked.

He shuffled in his chair and squeezed my hands again.
"Sure. What I tell my own daughters is that masturbation is a doing word, not a naming word. So, it's a sinful,
carnal action in the eyes of God."
"What's a carnal action?' I humbly asked.

He shuffled in his chair again. His face was getting red and his fingers
were rubbing my hands.

"Well Sister Gordon, the carnal action of masturbation
occurs when you take your own hands and touch your
private parts in a way that soils your gifts for your eternal husband."

He let out a big sigh. The answer must have been hard for him to
remember.

"Thank you. No, I do not do the carnal action of masturbation," I said with some relief.

Only Cedric and David had touched my private parts. But he didn't ask
me if someone else was touching me. He only asked if 'I' was touching
me so the answer to that question could only be 'No'.

"Very good. Is there anything you need to talk to me
about?"
"No," I lied.

End of interview.

I took a slow walk home.

My insides were all tangled up.
They were stuffed with too many secrets.

I could not tell the Bishop most of my secrets because they would get Cedric into big trouble. Cedric was about to be ordained a high priest and I had the feeling that his kissing lessons didn't count towards his priesthood credits in church or heaven. I didn't tell the Bishop about the worms because they had nothing to do with church and I wasn't sure they were gone. It had to be a secret until I knew for sure. I didn't tell the Bishop about my mother crying all the time because I didn't know why she cried or how to fix it. I couldn't tell the Bishop about what happened each time I went to the stock cars with David because it wasn't masturbation and my clothes were always modest and spotless. I couldn't tell the Bishop about not wanting to learn how to crochet because the Bishop was a man and would not know what I was talking about.

I couldn't tell the Bishop that I turned the Holy Ghost off sometimes. That would be really impolite. No one likes to be turned off. I prided myself in being obedient and in having pure thoughts. I wanted to be the best Sunbeam for Jesus. I tried every day to listen to the Holy Ghost but his messages were getting old. Be quiet and patient, be quiet and still, be quiet and obedient, be quiet and kind, work hard and fast, work hard and fast, be quiet and work, blah, blah, blah!

Bishop Morrison's interviews were getting old too. I was getting old. It was 1968 and I had just turned twelve and all I wanted was an ice cold Coca-Cola! That would be new. It would also be against the Word of Wisdom and my Sunbeam song. But I was in the young adult class now. Or was I? I had to check on the crochet issue at my next Primary class.

She flunked me.
She wouldn't let me graduate with the class the next Sunday because I refused to do the crochet project. For the first time in months, very bad thoughts began to form in my head on the front pew of the church. What happened to the points in heaven I had earned from all my sacrifices? Did they not count for anything? Good things come to those who

sacrifice. That's the deal! I left church early, walked home and sat in my room. I said a swear word out loud. I learned it from Jeremy, who had said it to Mother.

"Shit!" I yelled.

It felt really good to say a bad word.
No wonder Jeremy said so many of them.
I imagined the taste of Coca-Cola.
Cedric walked into my room.

"Gidday Pip. David told me in priesthood class that he really likes you a lot. How about you go to the hot pools with him on Saturday?"

Silence.

I was getting really sick and tired of Cedric fixing me up with David. It didn't feel good any more to be with David. He was boring and his face was all pimply. I never got to see the races because David would always put me underneath him. His only interest was kissing my face and being inside me. It was beginning to hurt.

"I'm not going out with him anymore," I stated. "His fingernails are always dirty!"

Cedric knew what that meant.
David had no character.
He stood looking at me with a look of disgust, shrugged his shoulders, and left the room without saying a word.

I hated the silent treatment.
I had no idea what he was thinking.
All I knew was that nothing felt good these days. I had too many secrets and Cedric knew them all. He knew exactly how to get what he wanted, whether it was what I wanted or not. He also knew that I hated going

to my interviews with Bishop Morrison because of the way he held my hands. It felt creepy and his hands were old. He also asked me too many personal questions about the outside of my body. As my judge, what was he really trying to say to me? Was I missing something? Why was he always looking for something bad to fix? He did tell me it was his job to fix my sins. Maybe he would feel better if I gave him something to fix. Maybe if I drank Coca-Cola it would be a sin that he could fix. Then he would stop asking me so many questions. Then he would stop talking to me every month.

Cedric would not talk to me at all.
I became invisible.
Cedric wasn't the only one who gave me the silent treatment.
I never heard directly from the Holy Ghost any more.
I couldn't tell if it was his voice in my head or my voice.
Sometimes I didn't feel like I even had a voice.
Actions speak louder than words so my voice didn't matter anyway.
My actions at school were top notch.
My actions on slave day were perfect.
If actions speak louder than words, I was sure I was just like all the other Mormons I knew. Perfect.

I did not feel perfect on the inside.
The Holy Ghost had left because I was infested with invisible worms and dirty fingernails with no character. Cedric knew that David Johnson had no character but still brought him over to the house to work on cars. Cedric had told David that I did not want to go out with him anymore so David gave me the silent treatment.
Cedric also continued the silent treatment.
Doing our jobs together was stressful.
He was mad at me and it showed.
He told me every slave day how much I had let him down.
I began to feel sick on the inside in the knowing that in his silence, I was being thrown over the banister to join all my broken toys.

CHAPTER 10

MATTHEW 6:33

"But seek ye first the kingdom of God, and his righteousness; and all these things shall be added unto you."

Being broken did not make me feel very good. The thought of drinking Coca Cola made me feel much better. The thought of drinking Coca Cola was a sin, a bad thought, one of those very tiny bad thoughts sitting forever in the cardboard dog kennel of my brain. I knew that breaking the Word of Wisdom was serious and against all I had learned in my Sunbeam class and Primary lessons. I also knew that keeping the Word of Wisdom was one of Bishop Morrison's monthly questions. I also knew from the kids at school that Coca Cola made your tummy fizz, your eyes wet and your tongue dance at the taste of it. My head and heart wars began.

Debates about what was worse, drinking Coca-Cola or having to confess my sin to Bishop Morrison would be raging in my head as I dusted the cobwebs from the slatted Venetian blinds in the living room.
As my Judge in Israel, Bishop Morrison was sure to disapprove.
Mother would definitely disapprove.
God the father would disapprove.
Jesus Christ his son would disapprove.
The Holy Ghost would definitely disapprove.
All good Mormons would disapprove.
But mostly, Cedric would disapprove.

Having discarded me for months now, Cedric continued to punish me with silence. He was still mad at me for not going out with David Johnson. I was mad at him for not telling me all that I needed to know about going out with David Johnson. So, we stayed mad at each other. My silence didn't seem to bother him. His silence pushed against the matchbox in my heart and his actions became constant re-runs projected in the back of my brain as I searched and searched to find the lesson.

The church teachings were very plain about obeying the priesthood. To disobey Cedric's priesthood would bring isolation. This was very apparent in his silence. My job list got considerably shorter as Cedric no longer enlisted my help. He would avoid me in the house and withdrew his usual special attention from me. He started cleaning my room without my permission. He threw away school projects from art class that I had hidden in my small clothing closet. He yelled at me to keep my closet clean and tidy and to dust my shelves. My relationship with him depended solely on my ability to obey him. This part of the lesson was very clear.

Cedric's silent anger screamed futility. It was futile to resist his authority if I was to be happy. This part of his lesson became more upsetting the longer I pondered it. As long as the priesthood and my brothers were one and the same I would always be surrounded by them telling me what to do, when to do it, why I had to do it, and finally, how I was to do it. I was so tired of being bossed around by Cedric every day of the week.
I felt used and very unhappy.
I felt used by the priesthood.
I felt used by everybody.
There was no room for my needs in my obedience.
There was no room for me to think of or have needs.
There was only room for everybody else.

Good things do come to those who sacrifice but the degree of sacrifice felt out of balance. I was tired of monthly interviews and metal chairs in the Bishop's office. I was tired of answering all those questions. Now at twelve years old, I felt tired of being watched by members of the church all the time. I was sick of being told what a good example I was.

Being a good example weighed too much. I wanted a rest. If only I could just stay in my room for a week and be left alone. I could get up when I wanted to and not be available for any jobs or anyone. I could be invisible; invisible me meant invisible them.
I liked that idea. I liked that idea a lot.

Invisibility never materialized. The more I worked for everybody else, the more preoccupied I became with the thought of being selfish. To be selfish for one day would break all the rules, no jobs, no sharing, no homework, no talking to my brothers and no people in my room, including my mother. At the top of my selfish list was the desire to taste Coca-Cola.

I had been mulling it over for weeks.
Planning it.
Saving for it.
Surveying the territory for it.
Pacing out the timing of it.
Sitting in Sunday school I would review the steps for it.
Imagine the darkness of it.
Taste it.

We were still poor. Everybody knew it. I had been wearing the same shoes for two years and hand-me-downs from my sister forever. Money was only given for one school lunch a week. Once-a-week money could buy a thick bread, black marmite sandwich and a shiny green sour granny-smith apple or two, jam covered, very large, cream-filled buns. The daily half-pint ration of milk from the New Zealand government was free. My ration to one bun each week would leave three-pence in change, and a month of saving to get the shilling now hiding in my one dresser drawer.

The whole world gets to sleep in on Saturdays, except for us. Saturday in our house begins at eight o'clock in the morning and comes to a weary halt at four o'clock in the afternoon, by which time potatoes have to be peeled, mutton started to roast, fresh milk found, table cloths ironed and benches set for Mother, my brothers and me and sometimes, most times, a stray someone from church. Evening plans seldom materialized because skirts and shirts always needed pressing for a full day of Sunday meetings, Mother and God's appointed day of rest.

Points in heaven were to be the only payment for Slave Day. A shrill call from Mother cut through the thickness of my eiderdown.

"Philippa, get up and get on with it!" pierced the
command.

Orders for slave day begin the instant the tired piece of white cardboard,
divided into columns of assigned tasks, is taped firmly to the old fridge.

"Early to bed, early to rise, up, up, up! If you want to
belong to this family, get cracking!"
"Ten more minutes," I plead in half sleep.

The eiderdown is pulled off with a jerk.

"Get your lazy bottom out of bed!" she says flinging the
top sheet on the floor. "You know the routine, nothing
happens until this pigsty is ship-shape!"

I'm up.
I'm freezing.
I hate her already.

Washing greasy pots warms my hands and freezes my feet on the cold
kitchen floor. Done. I climb up the window sash to dust the pelmets over
the window drapes in the lounge. Done. A small ragged piece of a large
tattered shirt wipes the coal soot into the cracks of the fireplace mantle.
Done. If Slave Day was done early I could make my escape from the ears
in the walls and the eyes in the bathroom door. The washing line turns
in the wind.

Firewood is stacked chest deep in the carport. Done. Brown coal hauled
from the sack to the hearth. Done. Maggots hosed off the rubbish tin.
Done. The nanny goat moved to mow the lower lawn. Done. The footpath swept. Done. Spider webs brushed off the ceiling of the washhouse.
Done.

"Rebecca, don't forget the vacuuming." she yells from the
open toilet.

"Don't call me Rebecca. I'm not Rebecca. I'm Philippa," I
reply.
"Philippa, don't argue with me. You know who I mean."

She flushes.
I hated her when she called me Rebecca. Mother would also call me
Gylian even though she was dead. The vacuum roars and I work the
areas of grass- stained, sea green carpet and hang the Hoover with its
hose neatly back on its bent hook in the hallway closet. Done.

It's two o'clock.

I never had time for friends. Mother made sure of it. Our house required
a relentless attack with all hands on deck. I crank the handle to bring the
washing line down to my stretch so I can fasten wooden pegs to family
sheets around the mast. Cedric is scrubbing the basement and Rodney is
invisible. Lifting the load to reach the wind takes all my strength.

At eighteen years old, Jeremy is all muscle. He slams the back door on his
way to his escape in a car with a friend. My black mark joins untidy rows
of marks and smudges on the job sheet on the fridge. The hands of the
clock above the kitchen sink shows three o'clock. One hour of freedom
and here it was. Take it.

> "Philippa!" Mothers voice catches my courage. "Don't
> forget to wash your smalls. You don't want to smell in
> church," she yells from her bedroom.

Washing underwear by hand was also a nightly ritual. Mother's sacred
Mormon undergarments were always hanging where the towels were
meant to be. I had dried my hands on them by mistake more than once.

> "It's on my list. I'll do it after I clean my room."
> "Make sure of it. God hates liars and so do I!"

I hear the backdoor open and her footsteps on the path. She's on her way to check on Cedric in the basement.

I quickly close my bedroom door. Outstretched hands slowly pull open a very squeaky top dresser drawer. My hand searches between the soft layers to grasp the silver shilling sleeping there. I run my thumb carefully back and forth along her silver ridges. It's now or never. The smalls can wait. I create a crack to allow my single eyeball to search for any sliver of Mothers shadow hiding in the corners of the hall. This was it. This is the plan. All clear. Go!

Door open.
Five paces.
Right turn.
Eight paces.
Left turn. Go past the kitchen.
Four paces.
Right turn.
Front door.
Easy does it.
Open the door.
Look left.
Look right. Look left again.
Don't forget to scan the driveway.

My mother was known to spend endless amounts of time raking the length of our sixty-foot, rose bush lined gravel driveway pushing and pulling every small stone back to the center. Mother thought center was safe. Nothing sat on the edge in our house.

Rebecca never went to the edge of the world to follow her dream of digging stuff up.

> "Why didn't you go?" I asked.
> "Because I had to look after you lot. Who do you think changed your nappies!"

Mother needed Rebecca to be a babysitter so digging gardens became her replacement dream, her that'll-have-to-do dream.

I was going to make my dream happen today.
Get on with it.
No sight of her.
All clear.
I was a fast runner and it took my speed and my worn leather Roman sandals two minutes to arrive at the local dairy two hundred yards up the street.

Standing in the line my stomach fills with the sweet smell of licorice and aniseed, gob stoppers and hokey pokey, fresh bread and hot pastry wrapped meat pies. Scanning the two small tables in the corner window, I saw no one from church. Straining on tiptoes to stand taller and bolder at the counter, I plunked my shilling down hard on the high wooden top.

> "Gidday, what can I get ya?" the bloke bellowed from the
> other side.

The small shop offered ice creams in a cone for sixpence, fresh cream for less than two shillings, an assortment of chocolates for a penny, chocolate covered orange *Jaffa's* for a halfpenny, *Banana Bike* filling pullers for tuppence, and my favorite peppermint *Minties* for three-pence. I kept to the plan.

> "I'd like a bottle of Coca-Cola please?" came my rehearsed
> response.
> "For here or to take away mate?"
> "For here please," I answered with conviction.
> "Small or large mate?" he shouted, bending down to the
> lower shelf.
> "Small please. And may I have it off the ice," I added
> with the emphasis of flipping the silver head of the
> Queen over on the counter.

Thump, the large metal handle of the icebox unlatched. The stainless steel door sailed slowly open. Work worn fingers floated the green-glass bottle with the distinctive white lettering and red cap to the opener. I push my shilling across the counter and look expectantly for change.

"No change mate," came the mumble as he slid the bottle into my waiting open hand.

With two hands clasped tightly to the frosty curved dream in a bottle, I made my way to the table beside the shelves that held fresh baked bread. Sliding gently into the seat I tried to look like I was a regular Coca-Cola drinker. I hooked my left elbow on the back of the wooden chair so my arm and hand swing free and limp. I cross one leg over the other to let on to the fact that I was a 'regular' and that 'regular' Coca-Cola off the ice was my 'regular' drink of choice. My nose tickled as the bottle came close to my lips. Bubbles rushed past my teeth and danced across my tongue. My eyes watered instantly and my teeth closed tight together. I remembered this reaction to this kind of drink on the Spencer's black and white television set. The cowboy, with teeth clenched, a tight jaw and a hard swallow, would slam the bottle back to the counter for another drink. It takes guts to be bad. I had what it took.

I was twelve. I knew that Jesus, in his wisdom, had big plans for me. He surrounded me with men in white shirts and polyester suits to remind me that I would be accountable to them for all eternity. Service badges glued to my Sunbeam sash showed that I was worthy to be a Sunbeam for Jesus. I knew all the words to the Sunbeam song and I had memorized the Articles of Faith and multiple verses from the Bible and the Book of Mormon. Obedience was my life force.

I was twelve. I knew that my body was on loan, that I was only its caretaker, saving its gifts for eternal marriage and processing children. God was to be first, the priesthood of men was to be second and obedience to my family was to be third. Private thoughts were sinful. 'Self' was a word only associated with 'selfishness.' From birth I had been systematically programmed to be one with the Mormon collective and the principles prescribed to be the foundations and demands for perfection. Simply, it was a matter of ownership. The Mormon Church assumed complete ownership and I was compelled, inspired and encouraged to embrace such an omnipotent landlord.

I was twelve and for a fleeting moment in a corner store, all of my being was held in a small bottle of ice cold Coca-Cola.

CHAPTER 11

MATTHEW 11:28

"Come unto me, all ye that labour and are heavy laden, and I will give you rest."

I sat in the dairy for a long time making sure to get every drop out of the bottle, which by now was warm from the heat of my hands. I slowly twirled the bottle on the table, enjoying my selfishness with each turn. At last I had achieved a good deed that was just for me.

Good deeds are debatable. What I felt was a good deed for me God thought was a bad deed against him. The Holy Ghost agreed with God and sure enough, the Holy Ghost feelings started to creep into my head and down to push against my heart.

Was the moment of fizzy glee worth the sin?

Was the taste of it worth the sin?

Was the planning of it worth the sin?

The slow magical twirl of my bottle was replaced with nervous tapping fingers against the green glass. Selfishness began to give me an upset stomach. My record in heaven now had a black mark on it due to the fact that my sin couldn't be reversed. There was no way to put the Coca-Cola in my stomach back in the bottle and in an instant sin was a headache and guilt became the real thing.

At least I had something for Bishop Morrison to fix. This would make him happy. Our next interview came; same time, same place, same metal chair, fourth question after the same masturbation question.

"Sister Gordon, are you obeying the Word of Wisdom?" he asked.

I knew I had to confess my sin to make my stomach feel better and my headache go away.

"No sir," I told him.

Silence.

He looked right through me.
I took a deep breath and spoke with a timid tone.

> "Last Saturday I went to the dairy and brought a small bottle of Coca-Cola off the ice and drank every drop. I feel really bad about it Bishop Morrison, but I had been thinking about it for such a long time. I knew I had to act on my thoughts to get them out of my head."
> "Sister Gordon, you do know that disobeying the Word of Wisdom is a very serious sin against your Father in Heaven?" he replied.

He made no reference to the fact that my own thought removal process had been a success.

Silence.

My mind went on a walkabout. I had drunk a thousand Coca-Cola's in my mind but I had only drunk one in the dairy. I did not tell the Bishop about the thousand in my head. *"As a man thinketh so is he,"* said a very small voice deep in my head. This was the Holy Ghost telling me how bad it was to break the Word of Wisdom. He had been back on occasion since Cedric had stopped his lessons with me.

> "Sister Gordon," Bishop Morrison said breaking the silence. "You are a chosen vessel of the Lord. I am sure that he is disappointed in your weakness last Saturday but God does understand that we are human and by our nature we are going to sin. This is why he sent his only

begotten son Jesus Christ to earth to atone for our sins. Do you know that Jesus was crucified for your sin?" he said with watery eyes.

Silence.

My mind went on another walkabout. At church I had seen photographs of Jesus hanging on a big wooden cross. He had prickles on his head where the blood was dripping. He had big nails in his hands and feet. His eyes were looking down. His face looked pale like he didn't feel very good at all. Now I really felt bad. I felt guilty that I had caused Jesus such pain. I could feel my face turn pale. I realized that Jesus was crying and nailed to a cross for my bottle of Coca-Cola. At that same moment I also realized that God the Father was going to punish me. God's punishment had to be worse than Mrs. Cheverton's kennel, Mrs. Lancert's strap or Cedric's silence. This was really going to hurt.
I shifted on my metal folding chair.
I braced myself.

"God sacrificed his only son for you," he continued.
"Do you understand what sacrifice means Sister Gordon?" he said looking sternly into my eyes from behind his desk.
"Yes, good things come to those who sacrifice," I immediately replied.
"That's right. Jesus sacrificed himself so he could bring the goodness of the gospel into your life. God the Father sacrificed his son to bring salvation to the whole world through his power and authority of the priesthood," he preached.

I knew this.
My brothers taught me this every day.

He continued his sermon.

> "Jesus wants you to obey his commandments as given in
> the Holy Bible, The Book of Mormon and The Doctrine
> and Covenants. Obeying the scriptures is fundamental
> to your salvation. You have been pre-destined to be a
> member of God's chosen people. You were righteous in
> the world before this one. You came through the veil of
> forgetfulness to be on this earth with a loving family. You
> promised before you came to obey God's laws. This you
> must do to be worthy enough to return to your Father in
> Heaven. Let us pray together to see what the Lord would
> have me do".

We got off our chairs and knelt on the carpet. He said the prayer.

> *"Our Father in Heaven, Sister Gordon and I come to thee today*
> *in prayer to humbly ask forgiveness for her sin. Please bless*
> *Sister Gordon with understanding so she may be guided by*
> *the Holy Ghost to live a righteous and clean life. Father, give*
> *her the strength to follow the commandments, and give me the*
> *wisdom to do thy work on earth. We thank thee for sacrificing*
> *thy only son for our sins. Please forgive us our weaknesses and*
> *especially this day father, let thy light shine down upon Sister*
> *Gordon so she may be filled with the spirit of repentance. This*
> *I humbly pray for in the name of thy son Jesus Christ, Amen."*

We sat back into our chairs.
He took out a gold pen from his top draw and started to make a list.
I sat quietly and waited. Finally he spoke as he passed me a large piece
of white paper.

> "Sister Gordon, the Holy Ghost has moved me to prepare
> this list of requirements for your salvation. Forgiveness
> comes through showing our Father in Heaven by our

deeds that we are truly sorry for our sins. Do you understand?" he asked.

"Yes Bishop," I replied.

"Thank you for coming today and telling me the truth. See you the same time next month. Please send the next person in on your way out," he said.

The interview was over.

This was the way God and Bishops fix things.

The list was long.

For a start, all my thoughts and actions had to be accounted for twice a month instead of once a month. I had to see the Bishop more often than I saw my mother. Secondly, I had to prove to God, and the Bishop, that I was in good standing with the Lord. This meant living all the commandments and proving it. I had to become more involved in Sunday School, develop more faith in my teachers, be more obedient, spend more time with my youth class, fast for twenty-four hours once a month and complete one service project a month. A service project might be doing extra chores for someone, visiting the old and the sick, helping my teacher with a project at school or doing something nice for my brothers.

The list went on.

I had to work on building a strong relationship with the Holy Ghost. This required reading scriptures every day for half an hour, saying grace over every meal including school meals, kneeling in personal prayer twice a day (more if needed) and attending family prayer twice a day.

End of list.

Bishop Morrison had given me no time to think about anything other than the gospel.

End of subject.

Being a freshman in high school made life even more complicated. Mother had enrolled us all as day students in the Mormon-owned and operated Church College of New Zealand. Just as the Mormon pioneers had reclaimed the salt flats of Utah and the swamps of Nauvoo, Illinois, the church purchased and irrigated cheap swampland in Hamilton, New Zealand. In 1958 the high school project was completed and the Church College of New Zealand (CCNZ) and a Mormon Temple were built on the site, blessed and dedicated to good use by the Prophet who came from America. Any New Zealand Mormon who was active in the church and could afford the fees sent their children to be schooled there. Mother was determined that her children would be no exception.

My schedule at CCNZ and church became complicated overnight.
I had to get up at six o'clock in the morning, say my prayers, get washed up, get my uniform pressed, eat some wheat-bix for breakfast and leave for the mile walk to the bus stop to catch the seven-thirty bus. The bus ride took forty-five minutes and cost eight-pence one way. Once at school I had thirty minutes to go to the library, read my scriptures or practice the violin. My mother had insisted that I learn to play the violin from her friend who would use me as motivation to get better at playing her violin.
I hated the violin.
My brothers hated the violin.

I became first chair in the school orchestra and was invited to give a solo violin recital. This is where I learned to cover my squeaks, flats and sharps with a comedy routine that included raised eyebrows and little hops on the high notes that made everyone laugh. My brothers never laughed. They slid so far down in their seats they were almost on the floor with embarrassment. I quit the violin as soon as I left high school and mother's friend became a respected violin virtuoso.

School started at eight forty-five with Devotional, which we were required to attend. One hundred day school students and five hundred boarding school students congregated in the David O. McKay Auditorium for the daily service that consisted of school announcements, hymns, prayers and two and a half minute inspirational talks given by selected student speakers. Once Devotional was over we went to our class periods; English with Sister Coe, a convert from England, General Science with Brother Petersen and History with Brother Bryson.

Brother Bryson was an American who taught all of us that the entire world was saved by Americans – always. Really? My father would have something to say about that and, as he was not here, I felt obligated to correct Brother Bryson regarding some salient points missed in his lecture on World War II. My only detention, ever, in high school came from that fateful day when I argued with Brother Bryson over my insistence that the Yalta Conference was not totally an American idea, nor was it the only initiative in existence for world peace.

Lunch was held in two shifts in the cafeteria where huge soup vats steamed with food. Fresh warm milk in stainless steel urns came from the farm cowshed that was operated by students in the agriculture program. In general the food in the cafeteria was palatable, more palatable than mother's food at home. After lunch I went to Music Theory with Brother Mason, a Kiwi teacher who always ate sardine sandwiches for lunch. Bending over my shoulder to correct my music notation became a competition for how long I could hold my breath so I did not have to smell his.

Physical Education with Sister Denton, a four foot nine-inch woman from Utah was always fun. My best physical routine was the rope climb because I was stronger, faster and weighed less than all of my Maori friends who loved to eat. Study Break was a full period of reading and doing homework that had to be completed if I was to stay late and work on the school play. Math class was the last class of the day and the worst class of the day. Brother Wilson was an American from Provo, Utah who would snort and swallow his snot in class. This made me feel so physically ill I dropped math in my second year of high school.

Classes ended at four o'clock in the afternoon. As day students we had the option to take the four thirty bus home or stay for study hall, do our homework and take the eleven o'clock late bus home. I often stayed late. If I missed the late bus my Maori friends would leave a window cracked in the dorm for me to climb through to be able to sleep on the top bunk in their dorm room. Missing the bus was a regular occurrence due to the fact that study hall went from six to nine thirty at night, after which I would work on the yearbook or school newspaper. Sometimes I had play practice that always went late but most times I just had no desire to be at home.

Home had become a miserable place.
Mother finally dumped all of Jeremy's belongings on the front porch so he would move out. Jeremy had got to the point where he was just too disrespectful to Mother. Cedric and Rodney ruled the television set and Mother was always out at a church meeting. She still cried herself to sleep at night and by the time I walked the mile home from the late bus she would be complaining at the fact that I needed to be home more often and that I was not to stay so late at school. There was never any concern that I was walking the street of Hamilton at midnight and there were never any questions about my work on the yearbook, newspaper or plays. Regardless of her lack of interest I did spend time at home when she was not there.

I was home on Friday night bath night. I hated baths.
I was home for Slave Day on Saturday. I hated Slave Day.
I was home Sunday for long church meetings and my Bishop's interrogation. His interview was still every two weeks as I continued to have to prove myself to earn my Coca-Cola forgiveness.

I was also home on Wednesday Mia Maid night.
Mia Maid class was something I actually looked forward to in my week. With only six girls in the class, our teacher Sister Pelton always took care to make special projects and lessons for us. Due to my diligence I was voted in as President of the class. Bishop Morrison would be impressed, as my life was becoming full of the gospel and my leadership skills were becoming honed. I was also given assignments to give two-minute talks in Sunday school. The first talk I gave was about the principles of sacrifice. I quoted scriptures about Abraham and Isaac, Ruth and Naomi, Joseph Smith and Brigham Young from what I had learned in Sunday school. These were the moments that I saw Mother. She always sat very straight in the front row of the church pews.

The *Plan of Salvation* was the main topic in Mia Maid class for the year. This was a large map that showed where I came from before this earth, why I do not remember this fact, why I am here, the list of jobs to do before I die and finally, where I am going when I die if I live true to the gospel. The map also showed where you would go if you did not live by the principles of the gospel – this place was on the very bottom of the map.

The *Plan of Salvation* told me that in the pre-existence I had chosen in my righteousness to follow Jesus Christ and his plan to bring us to earth to live the gospel, gain a body and develop faith. Some people in the pre-existence chose Satan's plan which had us coming to the earth with no free agency to choose right from wrong. These people became evil spirits, cast out of heaven and cursed by God to never receive a body. I often wondered where these people went and if any of my pre-existence friends were with them. I also wondered why Gylian came first and chose to die so young rather than go through the tests. I hated tests. I was not good at study and I always flunked my exams. Maybe she hated tests too.

Following Gods plan required me to come to earth, gain a body, be baptized in the one and only true Mormon church, get married to a Mormon, be sealed to him for time and all eternity and be sealed to my parents and siblings so that in the hereafter we would not lose each other. The *Plan of Salvation* also told me that my primary purpose on earth was to prepare for, seek after and serve my husband. Like Jesus Christ had showed us, Mormon husbands were destined to become Gods of their own planet if they passed the tests on this one.

To get to the highest Celestial heaven, Mormon men had to have devoted and invisible wives. Serving a Mormon husband also required having lots of children to bring other spirits down to earth to live a life with a good Mormon family. In all my endeavors I was to seek perfection, as perfection is our ultimate goal to gain eternal salvation and our own planet to rule. Once I was dead there was work to be done in the spirit world in teaching all those spirits who had not yet had the chance to receive the gospel. Clearly as a child of God in the Mormon Church my life was going to be just as scheduled in the next life as it was in this one.

Living the gospel consumed my life.
I had become a strong speaker and a leader in all my classes. As my work ethic motivated young people around me, I was called to lead special projects for the youth program. We began to complete projects in the community such as clearing trails, demolishing houses, painting roofs for the elderly and organizing bottle redemption drives as fundraisers. Most importantly, as an active Young Adult I participated in the baptisms for the dead program which took place in the Temple.

Sister Pelton told the Mia Maid class that all people of the earth need the opportunity to accept the true gospel of Christ. That's a lot of people, I thought to myself.

> "Sister Pelton, how is God going to get the message to all the zillions of ancestors who missed the opportunity in this life to be a Mormon?" I said.
> "God revealed a program which enables us to do the work for the whole world," she replied.

Now I had my work to do and would be honored with their work to do as well. Now I understood why Jesus created Christmas so we can all have a rest.

> "Assuming dead spirits accepted the teachings of the gospel in the next life, these spirits must have a baptism done for them on this earth. When you get baptized for another spirit we call it by 'proxy' or on behalf of that spirit. Sisters, this is a great blessing that through your service you give to our spirit brothers and sisters. That spirit now has a choice of whether to accept or reject the gospel and their proxy baptism," Sister Pelton continued.

It was made very clear to all of us that no non-Mormon soul can continue into any kingdom of heaven without baptism, marriage and sealing work being done by proxy on the earth.

This seemed like an overwhelming task. It was incredible that God gave Mormons the responsibility of record keeping for every soul that had ever gained a body on this earth. No wonder Mother was so interested in her family tree and no wonder Mormon genealogy centers and services are the most extensive on the planet. Names to be baptized came from Mormon families who submitted all the complete and correct genealogical records to the Temple for their ancestors to be given the opportunity to continue their journey towards the Celestial Kingdom. If names were not processed, your ancestors would have to sit in spirit limbo until the great Millennium arrived at which time the Mormons would be given another thousand years to complete the task.

Eligibility to do baptisms for the dead requires a temple recommend. Bishop Morrison interviewed me, forgave me for drinking Coca-Cola and issued me my temple recommend card. He was sincerely excited for me to be going and promised that after my first trip we could go back to our regular monthly interviews. Saturday morning came and I had to be at the church parking lot at seven o'clock in the morning to be driven to the Temple for an eight o'clock start.

Slave Day came second to temple work. The jobs on the list would be done once home from the Temple. I put on my church clothes and went out the door. On arrival, we were ushered through a special back door to a large registration desk where we pulled out our recommend cards to show the man in the white suit. Once passed for entrance we were led to a dressing room for girls where older women of the church called 'temple workers' helped us change into white baptismal robes. Everybody in the temple wore white floor length dresses with green sashes and green satin beret hats. We wore white floor length robes that looked like big dressing gowns, and special white socks so our feet would be warm and be quiet as we walked the hallways past closed doors and opaque marble glass windows.

Twenty feet down a carpeted hallway.
Down two flights of carpeted stairs to the basement.
Twenty feet to a large double doorway. Stop.
Quiet.

The doors opened together to reveal the most beautiful room I had ever seen. Every wall was painted like the Garden of Eden, the green carpet was warm and soft, the lighting was recessed and cozy, the smell was that of lavender and the room was very, very quiet. I sat on a metal folding chair and waited for my turn. In front of all of us lined against the wall on folding chairs were twelve life-sized, gold covered oxen standing in a circle as strong as a wagon wheel. Resting on their backs sat a large, round, deep, gold-plated elevated baptismal font. This font was not anything like the font I had been baptized in. This font was special. This font held water in which dead people could receive salvation.

My name was called.
Walking out to the font I started to get a little nervous. Holding on to the railings over a little bridge I finally got to the stairs that would take me down into the warm water. A man in a white suit was waiting for me there. Waist high in water, he showed me how to hold his hands and wrists. This was exactly a repeat of my own baptism. Holding his right hand to the square he began,

> "Having the power and authority of the Melchezidek priesthood I baptize you by proxy in the name of..."

There was a pause while he looked at his laminated waterproof sheet of paper.

> "... Marjorie Eliza Pigeon, in the name of the Father, the Son, and the Holy Ghost, Amen."

Down I went.

That day I went under the water thirty times for thirty different women who I had never known. I figured out in the van on the way home that between all of us five hundred dead people got baptized that morning; five hundred souls who could now accept the gospel and continue in the service of their Savior Jesus Christ.

I was no longer in the service of my brother Cedric or any of his friends. I had learned in the next level class, the Beehive class, what it really meant to be virtuous and chaste. I was taught the sinful meaning of fornication, adultery and incest. In these agonizing and uncomfortable classroom lessons I slowly came to realize that Cedric's kissing lessons and boyfriend lessons amounted to a terrible and unforgivable sin. I felt sick. I had participated in an ugly, shameful and sinful activity that now flooded my head and heart with guilt and shame. Cedric had abused his priesthood rights and our sibling relationship. He had committed a sin much bigger than drinking Coca-Cola.

He denied the truth of it by telling him and me, that his actions were just "kids-play" and that "I was taking this way too seriously." For all my service and effort to live the gospel, my little box in the corner of my heart weighed a ton. One of us had to take the responsibility and one of us had to be accountable for our actions in Heaven. I struggled to accept that even though Cedric had abused his priesthood and denied the seriousness of his actions, the responsibility and the accountability was mine to bear. All of it. There was not one piece of it I could let go.

I could not tell Bishop Morrison because my shame could no longer speak the words. Sentences and thoughts about his lessons would move down from my brain but would get stuck in my throat.

I could not tell my mother because she had no eyes for me. Sentences and thoughts about a daughter's love for her mother would move down from my brain but would get stuck in my throat.

I could not tell my twin because he had no ears for me. Sentences and thoughts about him saving me would move down from my brain and get stuck in my throat.

I could not tell Sister Pelton because I was the President of her class. Sentences and thoughts about Mia Maid virtue would move down from my brain and get stuck in my throat.

I could not tell my sister because I had no idea where she was. Sentences and thoughts about her abusive husbands would move down from my brain and get stuck in my throat.

I could not tell the Holy Ghost because he was only interested in good deeds. Sentences and thoughts about sending him away would move down from my brain and get stuck in my throat.

I could tell no one.
It was the only option that would keep my throat clear.
It was the only option to keep me breathing.
My only choice was to make the matchbox in the corner of my heart thicker and stronger to hold the silence of it all.
Which I did.

The more silent I became and the harder I worked.
In religion class I took on extra projects. One such project was to build a scale model of the Nauvoo, Illinois, temple which had been destroyed by mobs in the eighteen hundreds. I researched the building plans, room layouts and architectural details. I worked for three months and created a scale model replica of the temple. I researched the historical implications of the Mormon migration across the American Great Plains. I read accounts of Mormon persecution by mobs and tremendous geographic hardships on their journey to Utah. I read the heartbreaking journals of women who walked across the frozen wilderness pulling handcarts to Utah. I read accounts of families burying their frozen children as they moved towards the promised land of Zion. I had learned in religion class that the Lord only sends adversity to challenge and strengthen our

character. The Mormon pioneers must have had more character than any other population on the planet.

The project fueled my curiosity for history and fulfilled my credits for religion class. It also gave me tremendous respect for pioneers and especially any peoples who had been persecuted. I admired their sheer ability to survive against insurmountable odds. I became driven to read about other struggles: heroic escapes across the Berlin Wall, heroic survival stories from the Antarctic expeditions, the persecution of the European Protestants, the persecution and survivors of the Spanish Inquisition, the heroic struggles and defeat of the Native American Indians. My life in the library became immersed in stories told and contained in the non-fiction aisles. I was inspired by their sacrifice and felt compelled to try to make a small difference in my world.

Selfishly I was also comforted in the fact that my sacrifices and pain were small in comparison to those accounts of suffering and courage. So small in fact, that I buried my hurts through an unrelenting regimen in service to my God, service to my Bishop, and service to my Mother.

Chapter 12

Matthew 7:7

*"Ask, and it shall be given you; seek,
and ye shall find; knock, and it
shall be opened unto you."*

My friends were all Maoris.

This was much to the dismay of my mother.

She told me I needed to have friends of my "own ilk." I told her that I did, as we were all in the same class and we all studied the same subjects. I never really understood her position until one Slave Day I asked her about her South African experience. I was dusting the living room and she was polishing Nana's silver spoons from the drawer in the black Chinese dragon carved table.

> "Mother, did you have servants in South Africa?" I asked.
> "Of course Philippa, they all lived in a camp behind the main house and kept pretty much to themselves," she replied.
> "That must have been really great not to have to do any housework. Wouldn't that be terrific if we had servants to do all our cooking for us," I said.

Actually I was trying to make a subtle point with my mother that we were all tired of cooking meals. She looked at me with a face of disgust.

> "Really Philippa, don't be so silly! I would never have the houseboys cook our meals. I would never have their black hands in the white flour."

Silence.

I couldn't believe what I was hearing.

My mother was a racist, a religious, God fearing, tolerant Mormon racist.

My loyalty to my Maori friends remained true much to my mother's disdain and her constant nagging for me to spend more time with Susan or Victoria – the smart white girls. My extra-curricular activity in high school revolved around the drama club, the orchestra and being Editor of the yearbook and school newspaper. Silent in my internal screams, I found my voice in print. My editorials became fearless and my criticism of the student government was scathing. I noted that their petty politics over dance decorations were a waste of time and effort, especially when compared to the outrageous activities of our Vice Principal who was shaving the heads of students who were caught stealing in the dorms or classrooms. Clearly no one had informed the American import, Vice Principal Thompson, the Maori way – what's mine is mine and what's yours is mine too! By the time he was about to shave the head of another student he received an unscheduled visit to his office from my mother who had heard my ranting about the Thompson injustice at home.

Uninvited and at full sail she steamed into his office, sat down in a folding metal chair, and said,

> "Brother Thompson. How dare you bring these punitive tactics to this school and this country," she bellowed in full voice.
> "I am so sorry Sister Gordon. What tactics are you referring to?" said a surprised Vice Principal.
> "I am speaking to the act of shaving a young man's head to shame him in front of his peers. This was the tactic of Adolph Hitler. This is the tactic of disempowering and shaming and it will not be tolerated. We fought a war to stop this tyranny and here it is in its most despicable form. How dare you sir, bring such shame into our midst! I demand you stop this kind of punishment immediately and if you do not do so I will personally be taking my complaint to the Governor Generals office in Wellington and writing a letter to the Prophet informing him of this evil."

Stomping the tip of her umbrella down hard on the linoleum floor, she then left the office without waiting for a response. Mother was always an advocate for the down trodden. She was principled.

She had integrity.

She had compassion.

She just never had it for me.

Brother Thompson never shaved another head and most of the students were happy to see him return to America. I continued my schooling feeling proud of my mother for standing up to a bully and confused that my mother's racism was selective. Persecution and oppression of the Jews was intolerable. Persecution and post-colonial oppression of the African tribes was acceptable.

Persecution for me came in the form of New Zealand School Certificate exams, a compulsory rite of passage if you wanted to finish your last year in high school. These exams were three hours long in each topic. You had to sit at least four topics. My exams were in History, French, English and General Science.

Studying for exams was impossible.

I was too busy with the yearbook.

I was too busy with the school newspaper.

I was too busy with play practice.

I was too busy.

I flunked.

Failing my exams was a major embarrassment to me and to my brothers. This meant that I now had to repeat my junior year in high school while my twin passed his exams with flying colors and was now allowed to study for his university entrance exams. This was the first time in my life where my twin and I were now in different class ranks in school, a fact that he shared with me daily in his snide remarks about failing my School 'C'. This led him to telling me that I was too dumb to think about going to university. So I didn't.

In reality, going to university was not something I aspired to do. I was much more interested in going to drama or art school. Even though I had been in every school play it was a sad day when my vocational advisor Brother Pearson told me that I would never make it in drama. It was also a sad day because I believed him. Putting my first choice dream aside I settled on Plan B.

Plan B was enrolling in a vocational art and advertising program at the local Waikato Technical Institute in Hamilton. I wanted to continue my yearbook work in layout, design and graphic art. Being out of high school was great – no more uniforms! At my new school I could wear jeans every day, never see my brothers and do art projects all day. It was a class of eighteen rowdy, artsy and opinionated students who were all active in student politics and campus activities. By the second month of class I was voted in to be the class representative to the student association meetings held weekly in the cafeteria. I found satisfaction in being an advocate for student issues that needed attention. I was unafraid to speak up and with my church training I found that I could speak well to any issue on the table. This was an area in which I could make a difference.

By the end of the year I was voted in as the full time Managing Secretary of the Waikato Technical Institute Students Association. My design career would wait while I became a formidable student activist on campus.

My religious life was just as formidable. My activity in the church was unquestionable. My talks were expanded into other meetings. Two-minute talks became twenty-minute talks on doctrine, Mormon history and young adult themes of spiritual courage and determination. The Bishop told me that God had called me to teach the Old Testament Sunday school course for ten year olds. Saying no to God's will was not an option if I was to be a true servant of the Lord.

Teaching the Old Testament to a group of ten year olds was challenging. I did all that I could to make the bible stories come alive by adding extra scenes and dialogue. My excitement only brought condemnation from parents who were told by their children that, "…Jacob thought Rachel was a real babe when he stalked her hanging out down at the town well..." The following week God changed his mind about me teaching Sunday school.

I continued to be a regular temple worker for baptisms for the dead. My personal prayers were habitual. Family prayers were erratic because I was never home. My belief in the truthfulness of the Mormon Church was as strong as it could ever be. I held my beliefs close and shared them with anyone who asked. I held the little box in my heart close as well. It was still full of Cedric, worms and dirty fingernails and I continued to share the awful weight of it with no one.

The month my elected term at Waikato Technical Institute came to an end, I was offered a job to manage the second largest student association in New Zealand. Wellington Polytechnic was a multi-faceted program that included vocational training for industrial design, accounting, business management, interior design, welding, art and architecture, mechanical design and civil engineering. The job would require me to move four hundred miles south to the capital city of Wellington.

Leaving home was a matter of logistics. It was also a relief to be out of my mother's bedroom, away from Cedric's silence and Rodney's indifference. Rebecca was on her second abusive marriage, which I could not save her from. Jeremy had moved and was climbing the corporate ladder of marine insurance in Hamilton. My exit was fast and uneventful. One suit case, and a short flight to Wellington.
I was seventeen.

By my second term in office I was elected to be the National Secretary for the New Zealand Technical Institute Students Association. This organization represented one hundred and fifty thousand students nationwide. The President of NZTISA was Murray Pilkington, a handsome, articulate, industrial design student. Women could not hold this office and once again I felt limited by the power of the men in my life. This time it wasn't the Mormon Church defining my role but chauvinistic Victorian modes still entrenched in New Zealand politics. Issues of student housing, health and welfare systems, student bursaries and government grants were all on the agenda. Meeting weekly with the Minister of Education was an excellent opportunity for me to try my best to make a difference. Leading student protests, hanging off sixty foot walls for publicity stunts, living with heroin addicts for health studies and flying around New Zealand speaking on national issues became my secular life.

The direction of my religious life was noted on my mother's phone list. She had the phone number of every Mormon priesthood officer of the church in contact with me in Wellington – Bishops, home teachers, counselors, deacons, high priests. I dubbed her system 'Inter-Morm,' as just like the CIA or Interpol, her telephone reached out to every religious layer of my life. She was happy to be at the end of my spiritual phone line but she was never an active participant in my daily life. She never called. She never visited.

My respect for her was limited to my knowledge that she had raised five children without any financial assistance from my father. Her courage as a solo parent was unquestionable. Her devotion and service to the church was also unquestionable. Her pre-occupation to ensure all her children would get to heaven was motivated by Mormon doctrine, which told her it was her responsibility as a parent to do so. The strength and quality of family relationships were entirely predicated on our individual standing in the church. My mother would be held accountable to God if any of her children did not succeed in living the Mormon lifestyle. Mother was so consumed by the responsibility of this mandate she forgot to talk to her children about things that mattered.

Mother never talked to me about the importance of being me. She never told me bedtime stories or tucked me in at night. When I got sick she would close the door and check on me at mealtime. She never stayed in the room or held my hand to make me feel better. She never hugged or kissed me. She never talked to me about dolls or dresses. She never talked to me about the changes in my body. She never talked to me about boys and sex. These things I learned with Cedric or in the locker room at high school and at the stock-car races with David. She never talked to me about who she was or how she felt when she was young. She never talked to me about my sister Rebecca or my father or my dead sister Gylian. She never talked to me about why she cried herself to sleep every night. Mother only talked to me about obeying God's commandments.

In Wellington I was so actively engaged in the Young Adult program I had no space to miss anything about my family in Hamilton. There was only time for church and work. There was no time for boys or fun. I found fun in my work and I found boys to be boring. None of them ever came to the standards that would be judged by my brothers. This was a problem as Gods commandments and the Mormon expectation for a young woman is for her to marry a worthy man of the priesthood, marry in the Temple for time and all eternity (not just until death do you part), have as many children as you can provide for and serve your husband, the church, and your children for time and eternity. Marriage is encouraged to occur by nineteen or twenty years old. Unfortunate young women who do not marry by this age are generally labeled old maids and sent on eighteen-month missions where they are bound by stringent monitoring and schedules of proselytizing.

The moment I turned nineteen I was called to an interview with Bishop Haurangi of the Wellington Ward. Sunday after church I went to his office, which looked exactly the same as Bishop Morrison's office: a metal chair, another large desk and another Bishop behind it. I sat down.

> "Sister Gordon thanks for coming in today. I just wanted to catch up on your pursuit of excellence in the church. I know that you are very busy in the community with your youth work. We are all very proud that you're a leader of so many non-Mormons," he said without taking a breath.

He must have another meeting to get to because the next question was straight to the point.

"My records show you are an active young adult and that
you are nineteen years old. Why aren't you married?" he
asked.

"Well Bishop, I haven't met my eternal partner yet," I
replied.

"Finding an eternal partner takes some effort on your
part, Sister Gordon. You need to be more available to the
young men of the Ward and I would urge you to fast and
pray for God to send your man to you. That's all I wanted
to talk to you about today, just a little reminder that the
eternal clock is ticking and you should be having children by now," he said as he stood up, shook my hand and
ushered me out of his office.

Meeting over.

He was right of course. As a nineteen year old I should be married, I
should be having children, I should be advancing my home-making
skills, I should learn to can beans, I should learn to be better at house
cleaning and I really should learn to crochet. But clearly, first and fore-
most, I should be spending all of my spare time looking for my eternal
mate. My head buzzed with all of the 'shoulds' in my life.

It's not that I had been totally ignoring the problem, as I had been out
with lots of non-Mormons from work. We had a good time and there
was never any pressure from any of them to form serious relationships.
My problem with Mormon boys was the fact that, for the most part, they
were usually really boring as all they talked about was church, church
and church.

Mormon dating rituals are pedantic. Couples were encouraged to go
on group dates, or dates to church activities rather than secular events.
Dating in high school was discouraged. Simply, the dating ritual has
only one purpose; to find 'the one' true beloved whom God promised to
you in the pre-existence. Consequently, Mormon dates were often spent
in fervent prayer before the date, immediately after the date and for days

afterwards. Young men would pray for the answer to the big question, "Is she the one?" Affirmative answers came like lightning bolts from heaven, and God's instant answering service replaced long dating rituals with instant engagements.

I was introduced to Raymond Threadgill at a student association meeting at Waikato Technical Institute. An electrical engineering student, Raymond had a calm demeanor, kind and dull as ditch water. But what he lacked in excitement he made up for in tenacity. He was always around when I needed a ride or another hand on a project at the office. He showed interest in the Mormon Church and, as it was my duty to convert him, I did so.
I viewed his conversion as a gift from God.
He viewed his conversion as a ticket to marriage.
He began to talk about where he would like to settle and how his family was to be organized. "I want my wife to be in the kitchen in Whakamaru [*fok-a-ma-roo*]," he would say in a thick Kiwi accent.
I said nothing.

My job move to Wellington did not discourage Raymond's pursuit. He moved there too and got a job as an electronic engineer with the New Zealand Broadcasting Company. Set for a life in a predictable and stable career, he settled into the routine of work, church duties and youth activities. The good news was there were never any surprises with Raymond. In this respect I viewed him as a trusted, devoted friend. The bad news was there were never any surprises with Raymond.

Raymond finally, kind of, asked me to marry him. The subject slipped from his lips one day while we were on our way home from church in his car. He presented the proposition as a point for discussion rather than a formal question. That's the way he was. So, like dull as ditch water couples do, we discussed it, went round and around in circles and ultimately came to no conclusion. He dropped me off.

I just couldn't marry Raymond. "I want my wife to be in the kitchen in Whakamaru," repeated over and over in my brain. I was too young to die at the kitchen sink in the inland forestry town of Whakamaru. Yes I knew that Raymond would be solid, loyal, respectful, and all that the church required him to be but he was one of the shoulds. I 'should' get married and I 'should' marry Raymond because he said so. But I had no feelings or deep emotional connection with Raymond. In fact, emotional connections were absent with most of my suitors. This detachment earned me the nickname of 'Frigid Pip' at work. I attributed it to the fact that non-Mormon boys only wanted one thing, a girl to go to bed with. As an active Mormon, I never gave them that opportunity. By contrast, all Mormon boys wanted was a girl who was barefoot, pregnant and canning beans in the kitchen.

Kyle Huston was a member of our young adult group in Wellington. As my job with NZTISA was a twenty-four/seven occupation, the pressures of meetings and long distance travel often hindered my church attendance. Understanding these pressures, Kyle seemed empathetic to my hectic schedule and genuinely interested in my spiritual health and welfare. He would often make an extra effort to ring me at home or drop by my office just to say hello. It was on one of these lunchtime visits when he asked,

> "Pip, why don't we run away and get married for the fun of it? We could have a really good time."
> "Yeah, you're joking right?" I answered looking up from my desk with a smile on my face.

Considered sinful, elopement is not part of the Mormon agenda.
> "No, I'm not joking. I've been thinking about it for some time. I really like you and I think we should just get out of here and do it," he replied.
> "Kyle, I like you too, but not enough to get married, I mean, marriage has to last a long time you know," I said.
> "Yeah, I know, just an idea. Well, I gotta go," he replied walking out the office door.

That was the first and last time Kyle ever mentioned marriage. His parents divorced and at twenty years old, Kyle dedicated his life to looking after his mother.

Simon McPherson was a traffic officer and a very active member of our Wellington First Ward. I had brief, superficial encounters with him at church, but on the whole, I did not know him very well at all. One Sunday night there came a knock on my door. I opened it to find Simon, in full police dress uniform, standing in the doorway with a bunch of fresh red roses in his hand.

> "Oh my goodness, Hi Simon," I said on the doorstep.
> "Good evening Philippa. These are for you. May I come in?" he said with some seriousness.

I took the roses from his out stretched hand.

> "By all means, please do come in," I said in a state of bewilderment.

I showed him into the living room where he sat on the couch. The moment I sat down he began to speak.

> "Philippa, I am a good man. I live by the word of the Lord and I honor and obey my priesthood calling. I am here tonight because the Holy Ghost has guided me to come and speak with you."

I was silent.
I had never been in this situation before.
The Holy Ghost had sent him to talk with me.

> "Philippa, I have been praying about you for the last month. I have just finished a three day fast through which I have been on my knees in supplication to the

Lord. Tonight the Lord answered my prayers and has
sent me to you to deliver his message."

The room filled with the presence of the Holy Ghost. I faithfully listened.

"Philippa, the Lord has told me that you are the woman
in Israel that I am to marry for time and all eternity. He
has sent me to you tonight to ask you to join me in the
pursuit of eternal joy and happiness. He has spoken to
me through the power of the priesthood. Philippa, will
you join me as one with the Lord? Will you be willing to
be showered with love and appreciation as my chosen,
eternal mate?"

Silence.

My mind raced through all of my church lessons about 'the one.' I was
overcome with humility. His intensity was like a laser beam from the
other side of the room.
He looked good in his uniform.
All at once he was on his knees and sliding a diamond ring onto my left
hand.

"Philippa, with this ring I promise to be all you need me
to be. Will you be mine?" he said softly.

This was more than any fairy-tale could be!
There he was, my eternal mate in uniform unafraid to speak his mind,
unafraid to be gentle and giving.

"Yes," I quietly said, melting into the moment.

He started to cry. I did all I could to stay composed in the chair. He rested
his head in my lap. Looking up he whispered,

"Thank you, the Lord is with us. I will call you tomorrow."

That said and done, Simon stood up, straightened his uniform jacket, and headed for the front door. End of meeting.

Surprise! I was just swept off my feet by a traffic officer.
Surprise! I have a ring on my finger and a diamond ring at that.
Surprise! I was engaged.
Surprise! I was speechless.

CHAPTER 13

MARK 11:24

"Therefore, I say unto you. What things soever ye desire, when ye pray, believe that ye receive them, and ye shall have them."

Engagement to Simon consisted of attending scripture study, attending Sunday school classes and saying lots of prayers. For special occasions we would go for a drive. We mostly talked about church and his job with the police force. Finally the day came when he invited me to his home for dinner, an event which he had spent all day preparing. It was a dress-up affair so I put on my favorite herringbone jacket, velvet skirt and vest. He collected me at seven o'clock sharp and took me through the narrow streets of Khandallah to his flat, the back of an old Victorian wooden house that was built into the side of the hill.

Simon lived in a simple, one bedroom flat that was cluttered with piles of sorted magazines articles and books in overstuffed and full bookshelves. The New Zealand Police Force Gazette made one pile under the coffee table. His Bible, Book of Mormon and his Doctrine and Covenants scriptures were open on a side shelf. A small wooden table sat in the corner was set for two. Dinner was served. We knelt in prayer beside our wooden chairs where Simon prayed for wisdom, strength and devotion to each other. He also gave a blessing on the food.

The spaghetti dripped with his secret recipe for homemade sauce all day in the making. I appreciated his effort. I have no idea what we talked about; church and commandments no doubt, the usual dull Mormon conversational chitchat. By the end of the meal and I became quite unsettled and knew my internal alarm had gone off – I had run out of conversation and as I pictured my life with him in this place, anxiety began to climb the back of my neck.

It was time to go.

"Thank you for having me here Simon. Your spaghetti was really good!" I said.

"Thanks, but you should know it's all I know how to cook."

"Really, I don't believe that," I jokingly replied.

"Believe it sister. When we get married this will be your responsibility so don't worry, we don't have to eat spaghetti all the time," he said with ease.

He laughed.

I didn't.

It was the 'Raymond-I-like-my-wife-to-be-in-the kitchen-in-Whakamaru-syndrome' all over again. I excused myself to go to the bathroom.

Simon had a combination toilet/bathroom. Towels were neatly stacked and organized by color on the corner shelf and shaving equipment and skin lotions were in a straight row above the basin. I glanced over to the faucets on the bathtub. Resting on top of the hot water faucet was a black hairy thing laid out to dry. Being curious, I picked it up.

It was a toupee.

Simon wore a toupee?

When was he going to tell me about that?

He must be wearing one now.

How many more did he have?

I imagined our honeymoon suite covered in black hairy toupees set out to dry. I imagined running down the beach into the arms of my eternal beloved, my eternally bald beloved. Surprise!

Mormon men don't reveal themselves until they are engaged. Engagement means ownership. Comfortable with possession, they let their spiritual guard down to reveal the usual male desire for servitude. Simon had felt that it was imperative to fast and pray about me, but he had not felt it imperative to inform me that he wore a toupee. What else was I going to discover once we were married? Did he have false teeth? Was he completely hairless? Did he have a hairy back and a wooden leg? Our relationship was on such a spiritual plane we hadn't even kissed each other or been swimming at the beach. Until we were married I would have no idea what Simon looked like underneath his uniform. I returned from the bathroom feeling queasy.

> "Simon, could you take me home please, I'm not feeling well and I really need to lie down," I asked, trying not to stare at his head.
> "Was it the spaghetti?" he asked with concern.
> "No. I think I must have a touch of the flu so it's better that I just take care of it," I lied.
> "Sure but let's say our prayers first," he replied.

For the next week I prayed on my knees until they hurt. I read my scriptures searching for confirmation that Simon was the man I was to marry. The Holy Ghost said nothing. I received no spiritual inspiration when I thought of Simon. I was confused as to why God would tell him something so definitive and me nothing. Did God only tell men whom they were to marry? I was overwhelmed with the proverbial 'cold feet' when I realized how much I didn't really know or feel for this man. I was racked about what I had to do next.

I returned the engagement ring to Simon. I told him I was not ready for the commitment and that perhaps God had me confused with someone else. I told him that I did not have the same confirmation of our union and there must be another Philippa waiting for him. I didn't speak about the revelations in the bathroom because I didn't want to hurt him any more than I already had. My rejection of him was hard enough.

News spreads in the Mormon Church, so everyone knew the engagement was off. Young adults around us tried not to take sides by being silent. We were called into the Bishop's office for separate interviews and explanations. The Bishop noted that I had rejected a man of God and again he reminded me that my marriage clock was ticking.
I buried myself back into my work.

With my elected term as National Secretary coming to an end I had to look for other employment. I returned to graphic art and advertising by joining the staff of a local newspaper, where I would set up feature pages and lay out advertisements. The salary was low compared to the money I had been making in student politics. As a result I looked for a cheaper place to live. I started asking around the young adults if anyone had any leads on flats to rent.

After the Thursday night Young Adults meeting, my Maori friend Leah Mairangi offered to take me home. It was a windy, rainy Wellington night. I climbed into the front seat of her car and off we went.

> "You wanna go for a drive Pip?" she asked.
> "Sure, let's go around the Bay and see how high the waves are," I replied.

I loved to watch the ocean when the wind was up. We drove to Miramar Bay, where the waves were so high they were washing over the retaining sea wall. Leah was a skilled driver so we were in no danger of being washed off the road.

After some superficial conversation Leah began to ask me questions about how I felt about my life. We had known each other for some time now, but this was the first time we were alone to have a private conversation. She could tell that I was troubled. I told her about Simon, and Kyle, and Raymond. I told her I just couldn't do it.

> "What do you mean you can't do it? What does 'do it' mean for you?" she asked over the hum of the car.
> "Get married is the 'do it'. I know that they are fine, God-fearing Mormons who would sacrifice their life for me. I know that, but I just can't think about being tied to the kitchen sink all my life. I don't want to have fifteen kids," I said out loud for the first time in my life.
> "Yeah I know what you mean. I'm one of twenty-three children. My mother finally died in child birth with my

youngest brother, and you know what Pip, I really hated my father for that," she replied.

My problems felt trivial by comparison.

"Sorry Leah, I didn't mean to be insensitive," I said.
"Don't worry about it, you had no idea, besides, I really don't want any kids either," she said with some sadness.
"But don't you want to get married and all that?" I asked.

She let her head roll back with laughter and let out a loud rumble of words, "I don't think so!" Her tone was emphatic.

Leah was at least ten years older than I and by Mormon standards, an old maid. I wasn't about to ask her why. She parked the car and we sat talking to the idle of the motor and the whir of the heater. Then, for a while we just sat in the silence of our own thoughts and watched the waves pound the sea wall along the Bay. I broke our silence.

"Leah, I think the problem with me is that I haven't met a Mormon man that I really like enough to marry. They are all really boring. They pray about me and tell me that God tells them that I belong to them. Then I pray about them and I don't feel anything," I said.

The windows were beginning to steam up. Leah cracked her window to let in some air.

"Well, Pip, why do you think that is?" she asked.
"I don't know. Maybe I am not righteous enough to receive an answer. Maybe I'm not worthy enough to be married," I replied.

Worms and dirty fingernails flashed through my thoughts. Leah listened intently as I continued to talk.

"I know I should like them in my head, but my heart doesn't feel the same way. Actually there must be something wrong with me because my heart doesn't really feel anything," I said, as my voice began to crack.

My eyes started to water. Leah could feel my distress. She leaned over from the driver's seat and gave me a big Maori hug. Holding me as she spoke, Leah very quietly said,

"It's all right Pip, you don't have to do anything you don't want to do. If it doesn't feel right for you, then don't do it, and if you don't feel anything in your heart there must be a good reason why."

It was a relief to be with someone who accepted me so completely. She then added with a laugh,

"You Pakeha's, you always have to have something to worry about."

This was true, as in comparison to the Maoris we 'Pakeha's' or 'white dogs' were overly neurotic and uptight. I appreciated her attempt to lighten the mood in the car. It worked for about one second.

I don't know why I wanted to cry.

Maybe it was the absolute frustration of being so available to Mormon men, but so not available to them on an emotional level. There was no doubt in my mind that I was a catch for any aspiring single Mormon Elder. I had been trained well. So, here I was, parked by the ocean, admitting to myself, and Leah, that I wanted more from life than just a spiritual relationship. I wanted to be with someone that I truly loved. Was my desire too much to ask of God? Was duty and devotion to the church going to overshadow my simple need to know how it felt to be in love? Surely God did not require me to make this sacrifice as well? Tears began to creep quietly down my cheeks. Leah reached over and took my hand in hers. We sat in silence mesmerized by the motion of white wave caps breaking on the incoming ocean tide. The wind was up. Gulls with wings spread wide sat suspended in the constant Wellington crosswinds.

It was getting late. Leah put the gear lever into reverse and we backed out of the parking spot. She continued to hold my hand when she was not changing gears. It was nice to feel close to someone who cared for me so deeply. The car came to a slow stop at the footpath to my flat, engine idling as I prepared to make a run for my front door through the rain. Turning to Leah to thank her for her time and care, I was met with what seemed like the offer of another hug. Instead, she kissed me gently on the lips for what seemed to be forever. Lightning went through my body. She leaned back and put the car in gear. I ran through the rain feeling every water drop hit my face.

Sitting on the end of my bed I wondered how I should feel about being kissed like that by a woman – by a Mormon woman. My head couldn't deal with any of this. Perhaps I just imagined what happened in the car. Perhaps Leah had no intention of kissing me that way. Perhaps this was the way she kissed everyone in the Young Adult program. What was that about? My head ran in circles of confusion.

My heart was a different matter. For the first time in my life I experienced an amazing feeling. I had no idea what to do with it. Another 'it'. But this 'it' was powerful and this 'it' emanated from my very core. My head argued with my heart. My head tried to label it, classify it and dump it. It was a mistake that would be forgotten as quickly as it had happened. My head told me so. My heart lost the debate, so I tried to stuff the feeling into the already full little box in the corner of my heart. Life went on and I focused on my work.

It was lunchtime. I was the only one in the office when Keane Jackson walked through the door wearing a dark suit, white shirt, dark tie, and short blonde hair. He had been back from his mission for a couple of months. He sat down in the chair across from my large oak desk and immediately turned beet red. I braced myself for another revelation.

"Sister Gordon, I have been watching you since the first week back from my mission. I have seen you in your duties in church and I have heard you bare your testimony to the truthfulness of the gospel. I have been praying about you for the last month. I have just finished a three-day fast through which I have been on my knees in supplication to the Lord. Last night the Lord answered my prayers and has sent me to you to deliver his message," he said without taking a breath.

I had heard this speech before.

"Sister Gordon, the Lord has revealed to me by the power of the holy priesthood that you are to be my eternal partner. I have come here today to ask you to join with me in the eternal union of marriage for time and all eternity," he concluded and took a breath.

Thoughts of my conversation with Leah in the car raced into my mind. Looking into his eyes with laser beam precision, I spoke with the wisdom of experience.

"Well Keane, I'll give you two weeks," I said.

This was not the answer he expected.

"I'm honored that you would consider being my wife. I know when we kneel in prayer and ask our Heavenly Father, he will manifest all things to us," he said.
"I am sure he will," I replied.

He slid a small gray box across my desk. It had to be the ring. I opened it. The diamond ring sat beautifully in the box.

"Keane, what if the Lord tells me something different from what he has told you?" I asked.

He had no idea I had some experience in this area. He continued as if he had not heard a word of what I had said. Mormon men can be so arrogant in their self-righteousness.

> "Sister Gordon, please accept this ring as a token of our engagement. If we have faith, the Lord will guide us. I am sure that in two weeks time you will be assured as much as I have been assured," he said with supreme confidence.

Then again, for me two weeks was not a long time to sacrifice to find out if Keane was 'the one'. We arranged to meet after work the next day. He left to tell his Bishop and I went back to my office work.

Finding a flat to rent was becoming increasingly more difficult. Time was running out and I had not been able to find a place that I could afford. I was reluctant to answer ads for flat mates, as I had no desire to live with non-Mormons. Leah lived with Mani Wiapu in a shotgun house on Corammandel Street, which was over the hill from the church. Shotgun houses were two bedroom homes in which all of the rooms opened to a single hallway that ran the full length of the house. It is said that, if a father was chasing the boy who got his daughter pregnant, he could open the front door and have a clear shot as the boy ran to the back door. Whatever the story, these houses were cheap rentals and I wondered if they might want another flat mate.

That night the phone rang. I expected it to be Keane.

> "Hello, Pip here," I answered.
> "Hi Pip, this is Leah. Mani and I wondered if you want to come over for some fish and chips?" she said.

My stomach rumbled.

> "Yeah, that would be great. What time?" I asked.
> "Now, I'll collect you on the way to pick up the food. See you in a minute."

She hung up.

It had been three weeks since the kiss in the car. Much of my late night thinking time was spent going over the events of that night and wondering what to do with the feelings that surfaced every time I thought about her. I checked the list in my head: I missed Leah, I felt safe and accepted by her, I trusted her as a confidant, I knew we could become close friends, I knew she believed in the gospel, I knew she was a regular participant in church and young adult activities. The list in my head was comforting but when I thought about her soft kiss my stomach tingled and my body wanted to be held by her again.
How could I even think this way?
What would Keane think if he knew?
This feeling had to go!
It was unnatural to feel such things for a woman, and as quickly as the feeling surfaced, I stuffed it back down again. Clearly, the Devil was putting these thoughts into my head to pull me away from the gospel. A-ha! "Be strong," I thought as I changed out of my work clothes and watched for her arrival.

Screeching to a stop, Leah leapt out of the car to meet me on the footpath with a big hug. I hugged her back. We took off for the fish and chip shop on Te Aro Street, the best fish and chip shop in town.

> "How are you doing?" Leah asked with a big smile on
> her face.
> "I'm doing well. I got another marriage proposal today,"
> I said.
> "Boy, for a Pakeha you're really popular. Everybody
> wants to marry you Pip." she replied with a laugh.

That seemed to be true on one level. They wanted to marry the spiritual Mormon Pip. On another level, none of them were ever interested in getting to know who I was, or if I had an opinion on any subject other than Mormonism.

Fish and chips always taste so good. Large fillets of Pacific snapper, deep-fried in batter until golden brown, pineapple fritters, Paua (also called abalone) fritters, deep-fried fresh oysters and thick cut, deep-fried Kiwi potatoes for chips. We sat around the kitchen table and unfolded the butcher paper that encased the steaming pile of culinary heaven.

Leah's flat mate, Mani, was quite a character. Raised by her grandmother, Mani grew up speaking fluent Maori and learning English from the only two books in the house, the Bible and the Oxford dictionary. In her home small cuts were cured by packing harvested cobwebs into the wound and clothes were washed and scrubbed in the river. Consequently, Mani kept such a spotless house you could eat off the floor. She was also a formidable opponent in any word game, especially Scrabble. Mani worked 'on the line' at the freezing works (meat packing plant) in Lower Hutt, where she took great pride in the fact she was the only woman skilled enough with a knife to be on the line with the other butchers. Even without a knife, no one would want to challenge her on the issue. Picking a fight with Mani would not be a good idea; she was feisty, had a quick temper and was the most tenacious, defensive, stubborn Maori I would ever know.

Leah worked as a public bus driver for the city. She was a natural 'people person' with a great smile, an even temperament, an open heart, and a totally non-judgmental disposition. Leah gave to her world, and everyone in it, great compassion. She was not a taker. Leah was a giver and the only person in my circle of friends who was genuinely interested in what I thought and how I felt.

Eating fish and chips and visiting Coramandel Street became a frequent pleasure. It wasn't too long before they found out I was looking to move into a less expensive flat.

> "Hey Pakeha, why don't you just live here with us?" asked Mani one Saturday night.
> "Yeah Pip, why don't you? We have three beds and you can sleep in any one of them," added Leah.

"Nah, it's all right, I don't want to upset the apple cart around here," I politely replied.

Mani took offense, as it is not acceptable to deny a Maori the blessing of giving you a gift.

"Hey, Pakeha, don't argue. You just do as you're told. We'll look after you so you don't have to worry about anything," Mani said with finality.

"Pip, you really don't have to worry about it because it would be lovely if you stayed with us," Leah said in her quiet assuring tone.

"Well, I'll think on it and get back to you about it next week," I replied.

"Next week! Bloody hell mate, next week is years away! We'll come and get your stuff tomorrow," ruled Mani.

There was no more to be said.

Two suitcases and a box, move complete.

Living with Leah and Mani was great. Nights were spent singing, playing scrabble, talking, listening to the stereo or watching television. Both Leah and Mani were excellent guitar players and would sing all the local favorites in perfect harmony. It was easy living with no expectations, no rules and no stress.

Going out with my fiancée Keane was nothing but stress. He would put me on his elbow and show me off to his relatives, his church friends and his missionary mates. I began to feel like his trophy. Three weeks had passed and I was having difficulty in imagining why God would want me to be with this man for all eternity. There was no doubt I was getting cynical about 'the one', and poor Keane was oblivious to anything other than his own priesthood calling and conceit. By the end of the third week I told him I felt that we were not meant to be together. He implored me to fast and pray about it for another week and he would do the same.

Within the first month of living at Coromandel Street, and, much to my confusion, tensions began to develop between Mani and Leah. There were heated discussions at night behind closed doors. What they were about I had no idea. Mani began to act out by not going to church or the Young Adult program. She asked me to swap rooms with her so she could be in a room of her own. No problem. Sharing a room with Leah would be fine.

Crisis arrived at one o'clock in the morning.
Mani stumbled through the front door out of control and very drunk. She had gone to the local pub and drowned herself in alcohol. When Leah and I got up to attend to the commotion, Mani began to be violently sick. Her breathing was erratic. Leah took control and told me to get on the other side of her. We held Mani up under her arms and began walking.

For two hours we did nothing but walk her up and down the street in an attempt to sober her up. Mani's breathing began to normalize, and finally the need for sleep began to replace her nausea. We helped her into Leah's bed. Fully clothed, Leah lay beside her to wait for sleep. I lay fully clothed and exhausted on the other bed. Quiet, calm and sleep came.

I awoke with the touch of Leah's arm across my back. She had left Mani to sleep off her drunken stupor and had thrown a blanket over me to keep me warm. Thinking I was asleep, she snuggled in beside me. She held me with her arm. I felt her breathing on the back of my shoulder. I wanted to turn around to her and hug her back. Instead, I lay frozen, trying to control my wish to hold her, trying to snuff out my desire to be held and kissed by her soft lips again. She began to breath deep with rest as my heart and my head went into full-scale war.
'As a man thinketh, so is he.'
I want to hold her.
'Actions speak louder than words.'
Resist the temptation.
'You are a child of God.'
Be virtuous and obedient.
'Carnal desires are of the devil.'

Being here feels so natural and so right.
'The Holy Ghost will manifest the truth unto you.'
But this is my truth, and my truth is real.

My feelings, now rushing to the surface, were as real and alive as the wind and waves of the ocean. Pushing against the tides of 'shoulds' for the first time in my life I gave myself permission to hold and feel my own truth.

Turning slowly toward Leah I gently rested my head on her shoulder. She stirred in half-sleep and adjusted her body to cradle me in her arms. Her cheek came close to mine and our lips slowly found each other. A small soft kiss grew into deep passion of mutual desire, and the awareness of the world outside of our own wants, vanished.

CHAPTER 14

MATTHEW 7:1

"Judge not, that ye be not judged."

◇ ◇ ◇

Three years of tormenting contradictions had brought me to where war ravaged my head and heart. My feelings for Leah were so visceral I could not dismiss the reality of their power. Simultaneously, guilt and fear of God's retribution racked my soul and besieged my testimony of the gospel. Survival became a dangerous dance between submission and service; submission to my feelings and service to the church to atone for them.

Leah and I spent as much time as we could together. At every opportunity we found each other's arms. Our love for each other grew in the safety of the little house on Coramandel Street. We continued to attend church every Sunday and the Young Adults program every Thursday, but church activities became harder to endure as our glances transformed into knowing looks of intimacy. Our platonic touches, now wanting to be warm caresses, became guarded. Shoulds and wants became imbalanced; feeling and thought fought in the numbing of my heart. Self-destruction and guilt finally overwhelmed any loyalty to my own awareness, as I stuffed and folded my desire inward to be shelved with worms and dirty fingernails.

Living a double life began to kill me from the inside out. Symptoms of my disease were initially manifested by the inability to look at myself in the mirror without feeling profound shame. Personal care began to slip away under the guise of seventies grunge and unconditional acceptance. Self-awareness became locked in a prison in which I could not speak. My circle of Mormon friends slowly disappeared, as appointments, meetings and dates were purposely forgotten or avoided. Ambition gave way to living each day as it came with little thought, plans or schedules. Elation would come at night in the arms of my beloved and condemnation would come each morning as I practiced the rituals of self hate.

My fiancée, Keane Jackson, never had a chance to go beyond my two-week stipulation. Despite the return of the ring, Keane continued his pursuit. I continually conveyed to him that the Lord had not manifested to me the rightness of our union. Keane continued to wait for me after church armed with excuses to walk me home. Ten minutes of stilted conversation, inner turmoil and disconnection filled my brain with a myriad of questions. Why was he was not listening to the Holy Ghost? Was his armor of self-righteousness so thick he could not feel my hostility towards him? When would God tell him that I was having a relationship with a woman? I desperately needed to get rid of Keane's unwanted and unwelcome attention.

Keane knocked on the front door, as he had done every month for the last six months. Regularity was one of his defining attributes.

> "Hi Keane, what brings you this way today?" I asked.
> "Well I was just over the hill at a priesthood meeting and I thought I may as well drop by on my way to the bus stop. Do you have a second?" he asked.
> "Um, well, I don't know, I'm expecting to picked up any minute," I replied, trying to think of exit strategies.
> "Oh, well, look I really need to share something of great importance with you. Can we talk until your ride comes?" he responded.

Lies never work and like a boomerang, they always come back at you. As my ride was fiction, "any minute" was going to be as long as Keane needed my attention.

> "Yeah, but let's sit out on the front wall," I said with some resignation as I walked to the footpath.

He followed close behind. Leaning against the low wall with his arms folded, he turned his face to mine with a look of humble desperation.

> "Philippa, I have prayed and fasted with all my heart about our union. I have counseled with my Bishop and my Stake President as to what I need to do to deserve your commitment. I know with all my heart and mind that you are to be mine. Please give me an opportunity to erase any doubts you may have about my willingness to honor and serve you as my chosen wife and mother in Israel," he begged.

I swung my leg over to straddle the wall. Looking intently into his bright blue eyes I had to put him out of his misery.

> "Keane, I really appreciate your caring spirit, patience and willingness to be my husband," I began.

Straightening his shoulders, he turned and straddled the wall as I had done. I continued,

> "I know that you have represented your feelings and rep-resented the feelings of the Lord with all your might and heart. I know that we have great work to do on this earth and in the next life to come."

He reached over and placed his hand over mine. I continued,

> "But, Keane, you need to know that Satan is sitting right here."

I placed my free hand firmly on my left shoulder.

> "I feel his presence Keane. I know for a fact that he is in full control of my spirit. As a missionary of the Lord, you

are in great danger. We both know the power of Satan and we both know you cannot be in his presence."

Keane withdrew his hand and climbed off the wall. His face had drained of any color and his hands began to quiver, as fear overcame his countenance. I waited for his prescribed response.

"I will pray for you," he whispered with a stunned stare.

I sat on the wall and watched him slowly disappear around the corner. As expected, I never saw him again and thankfully, my revelation finally ended Keane's misery. My own misery, now one with my shadow, followed me off the wall and back into the house.

Some months later Mother announced in a letter that she was coming to Wellington to visit. Reading between the lines it was apparent she was only coming to Wellington to survey my spiritual wellbeing. A few months earlier Leah had called my mother to ask her to come to Wellington at once. An ovarian cyst, traveling through my system, brought incredible pain and muscle shock. Doubled over and barely conscious, I had been bundled into a taxi by Leah and Mani and carried up the hospital steps to intensive care. Calling from the telephone in the emergency room, Leah informed Mother of the situation in the expectation she would come to Wellington immediately. Mother's response was one of indifference. She instructed Leah to summon the Elders to the hospital to give me a healing blessing. She also instructed Leah to tell me that if I was living the gospel to its fullest these trials and tribulations would not occur.
End of conversation.

Obviously Inter-Morm had kept my mother informed of my inactivity in the church. Inter-Morm also conveyed concern about the fact that I was living with two inactive Mormon Maoris of 'questionable morals'. She had also been in contact with Raymond, my ever-faithful forlorn ex-boyfriend. Wanting to be with her own ilk, Mother had made arrangements with Raymond to be her accommodation and chauffeur service for the weekend.

Mother landed.
Half-an-hour later she was on my doorstep insisting I attend church with her that Sunday. As usual, I was not given the chance to disobey her edict or move the appointment.

Mother was always on the move.
Our conversations were never still moments of intentional communication. Her admonitions were acrimonious and swift. We lean into the crosswind from the Southern Ocean and begin the half-mile march down the hill to church. Already, my Sunday shoes begin to blister and the bugs begin to fly. Her strained, high-pitched voice slaps against my shadow.

> "Philippa! You have to get away from those girls!" she shouts. "They're a no-good bunch of Maori's and I fail to understand why on earth you would want to associate with such riff-raff! Really, I thought you knew better than this."

I slow my walk unwilling to keep her relentless pace.
One step behind, my reply finds her ears and misses her heart.

> "Mother, they are my friends. I love them," I reveal for the first time to the wind.
> "Don't be ridiculous. You are not one of them," she snaps.

I am two paces behind and maneuver to miss her shaming glance.

Judgment had no room in their tiny shotgun house on Corammandel Street. Cleanliness is next to godliness and Mother could eat off their kitchen floor. Fresh baked Maori bread, the sun bleached smell of clean fresh flannel sheets, unspoken rules never found or broken, gentle brown hands warm and singing slowly across my freckled back, Maori whispers pulling me into the same breath of a night long embrace. They were also Mormons so how could she possibly object?

Every Sunday, Mormons have the opportunity to take the sacrament (communion). Bread is broken and blessed. Water is poured into little paper cups and blessed. Signifying the blood and body of Christ, the bread and water is passed to the congregation. Partaking of the sacrament is a sign to your Heavenly Father, and all those who can see you in the church pew, that you are living the commandments of the gospel. This ritual renews your contract with God for another week. Refusing the sacrament immediately sends up a flare of spiritual distress, which in turn, automatically raises a red flag in heaven, as well as the eyebrows of ever watchful newly appointed Bishop Merrick.

We were sitting in the third row (Mother liked to be seen) center; the sacrament tray came down the pew from my right. First was the bread. I passed it on. Mother offered it back to me. I pushed it away. The water tray came from the same direction. I passed it on. Mother swallowed hard, dumped the disposable tiny empty cup in the center hole of the tray, let out a sigh of disgust, and shot a sideways glance in my direction. My eyes slid downward and followed the patterns of the linoleum floor. I felt my guilt and shame begin to sneak out the pores in my skin. My face strained with the weight of my sins. At this moment the last place I wanted to be was sitting next to my mother in a church service that seemed never to end.

I waited outside the chapel while Mother talked to the Bishop. This was typical and of no surprise. She would be gone by late afternoon and my spiritual welfare would be back on the shelf where I had put it. Half an hour later she finally walked out of the front door. We began the journey to Coramandel Street where she would be picked up by Raymond and taken to the airport. We began the journey to Coramandel Street where I would finally stand up to the blindness and battering of my own Mother.

"Philippa, the Bishop informs me that you are not attend-ing your meetings. What's going on down here?" she probed.

"Nothing. I am busy and often away, so I can't be at church as much as I would like to be," I replied.

"Well, that not the story I am getting from Raymond," she snipped.

"Raymond doesn't know shit!" came my rapid response.

"Philippa! Don't talk to me using that crude language. You've been living with those crass Maoris too long!" she said.

"I have not! I learned to swear at my job, not at my house, and for your information, my Maori mates don't swear and they are far from crass!" I defiantly replied.

I was tired of Mother's racist little digs and I was determined that she was not going to get away with them any longer.

"Look Philippa," she said, "It is very clear to the Bishop, and to me, that you have become a different person. You look terrible, you don't wear makeup anymore, your hair is untidy, you swear like a sailor, you dress like a boy and you're acting just like them, an absolute ungrateful little bitch! What's wrong with you? Don't you realize that your Heavenly Father loves you? He doesn't want you to be with unrighteous people who have nothing to offer you, I mean their culture and your culture has nothing in common. I don't understand your attachment to these women!" she replied.

My ears had closed after the word 'bitch'. I couldn't believe that my mother had just called me a bitch. My ears pricked open again at her last words, "attachment to these women."

"Mother, I am attached to these women. They are my friends and they love me for exactly who I am. They're generous, caring and would give me the shirt of their backs if they had too," I said.

"Don't talk such rubbish Philippa. Don't you see they just want you to be like them so they can control you! Really Philippa, it's all very odd and unnatural for you to be around them. Where do you sleep in that little house? Do you have a room of your own?

"No, I share a room with Leah. What's so unnatural about that? You and I shared a room for years," I replied.

"Don't be absurd Philippa! Our sharing a room has nothing to do with anything so, do not let these girls cloud your mind. Besides, Bishop Merrick told me very strongly that the relationship between those two girls is known to be not normal. No daughter of mine should be near such people," she replied with her usual snobbery.

We turned the corner to go over the hill.
I shot back.

"Since when have you ever cared enough about me to start dictating who I should be around? Leah and Mani have done more for me than you ever have! Besides, you don't even know who I am. All you worry about is whether I'm a good little Mormon who pays her tithes and prays to the great white God!"

"Don't you dare be so disrespectful to the Lord. And those Maoris have done nothing for you, nothing. How dare you be so ungrateful for all that I have sacrificed, by the sounds of it you have become just like them."

"What's wrong with that?" I sneered back.

"Philippa, how disgusting to even think of such a thing. Obviously, you have become nothing but an evil, dirty little whore!" she yelled.

We had reached the front wall of the house. Lionel Ritchie's hit song on American Top Forty wafted from the radio and rolled out of the open front window,

> *...you're once, twice, three times a lady, and I love you...when we are together I cherish each moment, blah blah blaaah, blah blah blaaah, blah blah blah, blah blah blaaah, you're once, twice, three times a lady, and I lo o o v e you oooh...*

Mother refused to see my bedroom so she waited in the front room while I called Raymond to come and pick her up. She eyeballed the Lava lamp, the cassette shelf, the Maori carving on the wall and the cushions on the floor. I escorted her back out to the footpath to wait for her ride.

> "That house is a den of iniquity Philippa, full of Lava lamps and strange carvings. You get out of there and back to church so you can marry Raymond. He is such a good man and he still loves you so much. Your brothers are going to be very upset when I tell them about this situation. Don't you have any regard for the Gordon name? Obviously not, as you drag it into the gutter with this crowd. That's where you are Philippa, in the gutter!" she spewed.

I was still singing with Lionel in my head. It was easier than listening to the verbal vomit coming out of the mouth of my mother. Raymond arrived promptly and packed her off to the airport. There were no motions or words of goodbye. There were only the resounding words of bitch, evil, whore and gutter.

Bishop Merrick sent two priesthood men over to instruct me to meet with him the following Saturday at two o'clock. I sat quietly in my usual chair. My instincts oscillated between escape and rescue; the polemic power of denial pulling against the suck of spiritual quicksand.
My guilt held me tight to my chair.

I knew that the feelings so real to me were the very feelings that went against everything I knew and everything I had learned to be in the Mormon Church. The barrage of criticism coming from my Mother and now from the Bishop was crushing. The matchbox in my heart was so overflowing with secrets I slumped in my chair in absolute despondency at the weight of it.

I had no answers for Bishop Merrick. The words were once again stuck in my throat.

I had no answers for my Mother. Her venom had begun to erode my heart walls.

I had no answers for God. The light in my Sunbeam could not shine for him.

I had no answers for me. My heart hurt and my head spun with conflicted needs and wants, demands and commandments.

Bishop Merrick regarded the tears sneaking out of my eyes and falling down reddened cheeks as the contrite first step of repentance. He knelt in prayer to ask the Lord for guidance. I sat numb in my chair. I could no longer navigate my ship as I floated without a rudder, lost in the depth of indecision, lost in a squall of whiteness where sky and ocean have no boundaries. The only current I knew, the only lifeline I knew was to succumb to the forever infused fierce pull of God's will and Bishop's admonitions. My survival in the church depended upon it. Keeping my matchbox sealed also depended on it.
I broke.
Sinful actions and sinful friends needed to be removed from my heart.
Thy will be done.

A new course was set.
As advised by the Prophet and his twelve Apostles of the church in Utah, quarantine from the disease of undesirable relationships is the required first step back to God.

I was to have no contact with Mani and Leah ever again in my life. To assist the heart removal process I was instructed to plan a two-week vacation far from Wellington and preferably to another country where Leah could not drive to see me. It was decided by Bishop Merrick that I travel to Fiji for a two-week holiday to re-think and re-align.

I hated traveling alone.
The thought of discovering new worlds with no one to share in the joy of it was depressing. The fact that I had to sell my car to pay for the trip was equally depressing.
Thy will be done.

Being alone in a new world would bring new perspectives and spiritual renewal.
Thy will be done.

I was on a plane to the Fijian Islands for a spiritually required break from the bad influence of my best friends.
Thy will be done.

Fiji was dreadful.
Mother had already called ahead to the mission president in Fiji to make sure that missionaries and the priesthood knew that I was in the country. My fifth floor hotel room at the Suva Travel Lodge looked over an industrious coffin maker. The noise of the elevator combined with the window air conditioner did not permit sleep. There was nothing on the hotel menu, other than salad, that I recognized. When I ordered mushrooms I received squid boiled in its own black ink. When in search for fresh fruit at the open market, I discovered large oranges and an equally large, black and hairy spider that came with them. Equatorial heat was not my idea of a good time, and groping, shouting East Indian merchants made walking through the city more of a challenge than I could stand. I retreated to my hotel room.

By the fourth night I had made up my mind to fly to a resort on the other side of the island. The location was remote and my hope was that it would provide the respite I needed and the isolation I needed from messages left at the hotel desk by Mormon missionaries. It did not.

Nights were so hot in a room with no air-conditioning. I tried to sleep with just the screen door closed to my poolside room to try to get some coolness off the water. The mesh of the screen scratched all night under the little feet of lizards, frogs and unidentified species that scampered all over the walls. I hate bugs.

After a sleepless night of creepy crawlies I was desperate for rest. A cool ocean breeze wafted through the courtyard where resort staff had set up beach lounge chairs and tables for guests who like a book with their sun chair. Encasing my white Mormon skin in a light cotton wrap I made myself comfortable for a relaxing morning by the pool and the need for a nap. Five hours later I awoke to the sound of sweeping on the tiled patio of my room. I left the pool to take a shower, change my clothes and go in search of food.

The moment my eyes saw myself in the mirror I knew I was in trouble. My skin looked as red as a crayfish and the moment I took a shower I knew that the sunburn across my chest was severe. Without any sunburn cream or lotions the best I could manage was a cool washcloth laid gently across my skin as I braced for another sleepless night with bugs on the wall and the new sting of sunburn. Clearly before I received forgiveness the Lord was making sure that he left his mark on me. This would allow me to remember my journey. This would humble me before the Lord. If he could physically break me down it would be easier for me to see the light and salvation found in Christ.

Morning light brought relief from bugs and intense pain from blisters. My entire chest from shoulder to shoulder has blistered in the night from sunburn. The weight of a cotton sheet was unbearable and the pelting of water droplets from the shower was equally unbearable. I could not cool down and I could not place washcloths across my chest. It was too painful.
The noise of waking birds was unbearable.
The pain of being broken was unbearable.

The loss of Leah and Mani was unbearable.
The sting of blisters across my chest was unbearable.
Life was unbearable!

My sobs were do deep it hurt to breathe. Alone on a tropical island hundreds of miles from anyone who could help filled me with the depth of despair.
I prayed for help.
I prayed for guidance.
The Holy Ghost took vacations but he was not on mine.

The Bishop and my mother had no contact with me once the plane left the Wellington tarmac. Leah and Mani were distraught at the fact that I had packed my bags and left the house without telling them where I was going. I missed them terribly. I missed Leah terribly. The Bishop promised peace and happiness without her in my life. The Bishop promised clarity and new perspectives without her whispers. The Bishop promised spiritual blessings if I were to show God my commitment to a new path. Fiji gave me none of anything he promised. It only gave me isolation, heart sickness and blisters.

> "Hello, this is Leah speaking."
> "Hello," I said in a crackling whimper. I immediately began to sob.
> "Pippa, is that you? Where are you? Talk to me," she said.
> "Yes, it's me. I'm in Fiji," I replied stammering through my tears.

"Fiji! What the heck are you doing in Fiji? Don't answer that. You don't have to answer that. Why are you crying?" she asked.

Through my embarrassment and sniffles, I slowly told her about the Bishop and the Fiji trip. I began to weep uncontrollably when I came to the fact that I had third degree burns across my chest and was in total panic as to what to do about it.

"Pippa, come home so we can take care of you. Call Air New Zealand and change your ticket to be on the next flight out. Get some sunburn spray for your chest to help with the pain and don't wear a bra, just the lightest cotton shirt you have."

Leah was always so good in these situations. She knew I needed permission to do what I wanted to do. She knew I needed instructions to take care of myself. The phone conversation ended and I immediately called the airlines to change my ticket. The next flight left the following evening so if I left the resort on the morning flight I would be in Suva in plenty of time. The only problem was that the flight took me to Auckland, not Wellington. Close enough I thought.
Done.

I arrived in Auckland at two o'clock in the morning. The airport was deserted and there were no hotel shuttles available. My chest was on fire. Not knowing who to call I flipped through my address book to find the phone number of Monica Carol. Monica worked in a hospital and had been a Mormon friend of the family while I was living at home in Hamilton. She and her three children had stayed with us during her divorce from her non-Mormon husband. Desperate for help I made the phone call in the hope that she would be home and willing to take me in for the night.
She answered in half sleep.
No problem.
Her husband Jon would be out to the airport to pick me up.

It was a short drive and soon enough I was standing at the foot of Monica's bed explaining the events of the last week. She asked me to show her my sunburn. I slowly opened the top three buttons of my shirt to reveal the infected yellow mess that covered my chest from shoulder to shoulder. Jon ran for cream from the bathroom and Monica had me lie still on my back on the spare bed. My shirt was off and a soft towel covered my breasts and stomach.

"Pippy, this is going to hurt but it will dry up this infection and begin to heal the burn. I need you to be as still and as brave as you can," she said with her kind nurse voice.

She began to gently dab the white cream over my chest. The cold felt good but the slightest pressure of the application was excruciating. The last step was to carefully wrap my chest with a bandage to keep the surface from being torn or irritated by sheets and shirts. Finally all was quiet and for the first time in nine days I drifted off to a deep sleep.

I awoke the following afternoon, made the phone call to Leah to tell her that I was in Auckland with Monica and that she was not to worry about me. I also told her that I was going to stay until my sunburn had healed. In reality I just needed to stall for time. Time I desperately needed to clear my head and figure out a plan. Any plan.

Monica changed my bandages daily and under her watchful care the burned scabs began to flake off my skin. Monica also honored my request not to let my mother, or anyone else, know where I was. She understood my need for solitude and separation from all of my spiritual guardians. For the next six weeks I stayed with Monica and Jon and their four children. I helped as much as I could around the house to earn my keep but soon I would have to get on with my life as I could not continue to be their long-term houseguest and I had to get back to Wellington where I could be with my Mormon friends and check in with Bishop Merrick.

The call came on a Sunday. It was Mother, which meant that Inter-Morm had been busy tracking my whereabouts. Monica bravely told her that if she came in contact with me, she would call. Not wanting Monica to lie on my behalf I decided that it was time to leave. With much gratefulness and sadness, I packed my one bag and caught the Silver Fern overnight train to Wellington. Eight hours later and after an eight-week odyssey, I was right back where I had started. Or was I?

On the train, I had given much thought to my unhappiness. A quote from a high school speech I had given in Devotional resonated in my mind, *"...you are the Master of your fate and the Captain of your soul..."* Life had to be better than this and I had to make it so. With renewed determination to get off the roller coaster of my life, I checked into a single room at the Wellington YWCA. It was not ideal but it would have to do until I was on my feet.

Within the week I had a job with another newspaper in the layout and design department. The wage was good enough to start looking for a flat of my own, which I found in Newtown, a suburb that was close enough to church and far enough from Corammandel Street. My bag, sleeping bag and pillow moved in. I knew that furniture, accessories and comforts would come when I went back to attending church, paying my tithing, saying my prayers, studying the scriptures, repenting for my sins and living the gospel. Contact with Leah and Mani was through phone calls and the occasional conversation at church. I became intent and driven to return to the familiarity and routine of living the gospel. If I was to be happy I felt that I had no other choice.

My twenty-second birthday was a celebration attended by all the local young adults. Life was full of work at the newspaper and full of church work every night. My feelings for Leah were finally buried by the hectic schedule of righteous endeavors. Scripture study and prayer groups often met at my flat. My personal prayer and testimony of the church began to thrive. Leah and Mani had been erased from my radar screen and I began to refer to my years with them as my personal test of faith. Clearly, it was a matter of understanding the principle of opposition in all things. I could never know the joy of the gospel if I had not known the depths of sorrow and sin. Adversity builds character and, like the prodigal son of the Old Testament, I had also returned to the fold with regenerated spiritual strength.

Spiritual strength was an attribute in the Mormon Church that always made for a popular youth speaker. Consequently I was asked to speak at local, regional and national church events. After one such program a very handsome and charming young man introduced himself to me as Keito Thornsen, from Hastings, Hawkes Bay. He alluded to the fact that we had been in high school together. I had no such recollection. Regardless, after some benign conversation he invited himself over during his next weekend visit to Wellington. Wow, this guy was something and, by the looks of it, his hair was all his.

After some investigation, I discovered that Keito Thornsen was one of the most popular high school heartthrobs. I must have been too busy with the yearbook and the drama club to notice. At twenty years old, Keito now enjoyed the prestige of being the only marriageable son of the Hawkes Bay Stake President. Stake Presidents are similar in rank to Cardinals and typically have three or four Bishops under their spiritual direction. The fact that Keito was a handsome, educated, well dressed, articulate, and ambitious Mormon was a rarity in itself. To think that he might consider dating me was beyond my comprehension.

Comprehension landed in my living room the first time he kissed me. This was the real deal, the one, the man, pick of the litter, the King of the castle, the cream of the crop, the cat's whiskers, the cat's meow, the best of show and the chosen one of Israel. Hallelujah!!
He prayed about me and got the usual answer.
I prayed about him and got the usual silence.
Faith replaced fear and soon enough, after the standard request and spiritual ownership speech I said, "Yes, I would be honored to be your wife in Israel."
Insto-engagement!

As requested, I immediately moved two hundred miles northward to Hastings, where I got a job as a traveling salesperson for Hansel's Company. Since I was Keito's fiancée, his family was very kind to have me stay in their spare room while I waited the three weeks to move into my own flat. Had I known what was coming, I would have camped in a tent rather than be at the mercy of Keito's mother.

Sister Thornson was the most meddling, possessive, bossy woman I was to know. She insisted that three weeks would be just enough time for me to complete 'The Sister Thornson Home Making Mother-In-Law Boot Camp.' Mother knows best and I was to know exactly how Keito was to have his drawers organized, clothes pressed, shoes polished, room organized, cupboards organized, socks folded, underwear folded, sweaters hung, cufflinks organized, bathroom cleaned, towels arranged, slippers placed and meals prepared. I escaped to my room early to avoid reading the required manuals on canning, upholstery and childbirth. Keito often joined me there and we talked about each other's day. Actually we did more kissing than talking and it became evident from the wet spot left behind on my covers that Keito needed to get the marriage ceremony out of the way as fast as possible.
Ask and you shall receive.

His father made a phone call and two weeks later we were issued our temple recommends. We were on our way to the Temple to receive our endowments. Thankfully before we left I moved into my new flat where I was out of the grips of Keito's mother and into a space that I could make my own.

Endowments had to be received before couples could be married in the Mormon temple for time and all eternity. As the epitome of required spiritual rites of passage the endowment process was a prescribed program in the temple in which each member of the church received advanced doctrinal knowledge and blessings. The endowment ritual was to be witnessed by family members and friends in good standing in the church and current temple recommend holders.
Mother was ecstatic.

She met me in the lobby of the temple. From there she would accompany me through all of the ceremonies before my fiancée would take over the task of ushering me into the room that symbolized the Celestial Kingdom, the highest heaven of all Mormon heavens.

The first step of the endowment process was to go to the women's dress-ing area. Two elderly women ushered me into a small cubicle wherein I was asked to remove my clothing and place something akin to a white cotton poncho over my naked body. Much to my surprise, one of the women stood in front of me and started reciting a set prayer. At spe-cific points of the prayer she would touch strategic points on my body; my forehead for knowledge, each nipple for motherhood, my navel for enrichment, my vagina for childbearing, each of my thighs for strength. Consumed with reverence and respect, thoughts and feelings about my personal space being violated were immediately abandoned.

This is the Lord's temple and all things are purified and blessed in his house.
Faith sister. Faith.

I was then blessed with a new name. This was my God-given name and unless I wanted to be struck down by the Lord, it was a name to be known only by my husband. In the resurrection Keito would have to call my temple name. Wow, I hoped he had a good memory, as being stuck in limbo while he tried to remember my name could be a problem.
Faith sister. Faith.

Keith also had a new name but I was forbidden to know it.
Faith sister. Faith.

I dressed in my white robes adorned with green sashes and continued onward to the first room of three and the companionship of my mother.
Tolerance sister. Tolerance.

It took an hour to get through the next two rooms. Each room represented a different level of heaven. Each room had beautiful murals, drawn by internationally renowned Norwegian muralists. Every wall and ceiling depicted a perfectly painted world in which the blessings and knowl-edge of God's kingdoms were acted out and shared by temple workers. Many times spoken answers such as "I do Lord," were required and it was obvious that those of us who were new to this process, had to come on a regular basis in order to learn spoken and acted rituals of passage. Our group was then ushered to the room in which Keito was to be my partner. My mother stepped back. The moment came for him to take me through multiple layers of white sheer curtains into the Celestial room. These curtains were symbolic of the veil of forgetfulness experienced by every human being who comes down to earth. The rites of passage to go through them could only be performed by Mormons in good standing before the Lord and Mormons who were engaged couples or husbands and wives.

I stood on one side of the curtain, unable to see him through the layers on the other side. A temple worker stood with him to help him recite the scripted blessings to his soon to be eternal partner. Once complete my hand was placed through the slit in the curtain. The temple worker took our right hands and placed them in a handshake position with our pinky fingers interlocked and our pointer fingers resting on each other's wrist pulse. This was the secret handshake to heaven.

Keith's voice whispered from the other side of the veil.

> "Alice, I call thy name to enter the kingdom of heaven for time and all eternity."

Gently, Keith pulled me through the veil into the Celestial Room, the grandest and largest room on the top floor of the building.

The Celestial room glowed with crystal chandeliers that softly lit gilded furniture framed by soft satin drapes and tassels to the sides of tall marble thin glazed windows. Plush carpet and French embossed wallpaper completed the austerity of the room. Green and white robed saints mulled about with hushed whispers and hugs. My world was running in slow motion as my eyes floated from person to person in the room. I was aware of Mother and her friends, Keito and his parents but not much else. My mind was back at the veil.

My mind was back at the handshake.

How could my life of obedience and sacrifice come down to knowing a secret handshake? Had the depth of God's love and the writings of the prophets culminated in knowing a handshake? Is the greatness of God's love predicated on a handshake? Scriptures appeared in my mind.

*"Come unto me ye heavy laden and I will give thee rest...*only if you know the secret handshake."

From the Beatitudes;

*"Blessed are the meek, for they shall inherit the earth...*only if they know the secret handshake."

How is it that my life of learning the ways of Christ was meaningless without the one and only key to heaven? Was this some kind of cruel heavenly joke? Who is this Mormon Jesus who needs a sign, a secret handshake to accept his children into the heaven he promised to them through the ages?

My questions would have to wait.
Keito nudged my elbow on the way past my stare. He and his parents were leaving. I stuffed my thoughts and forced my focus back into the room. Unaware that everyone had left, I stood alone in God's Celestial presence.
I stood alone.
I stood unworthy with questions, doubts and confusion.
I stood in the dressing room in bewilderment of my new knowledge, my new name and my God given secret celestial handshake.

CHAPTER 15

PHILIPPIANS 4:6

*"Be careful for nothing; but in everything
by prayer and supplication with
thanksgiving let your requests be
made known unto God."*

T wo weeks later I sat in my Hastings condominium resting after a busy workday on the road. My phone ringing pierced the peace of my living room.

"Hello, this is Pip," I answered.
"Hello Pippa, I found you at last! How the heck are you?"

It was Leah. Tears began to well up in my eyes from a place in my heart where I had buried my matchbox in cement.

"Hi, how are you? Where are you?" I asked nervously.
"I'm here in Hastings. I've come to see you. I'll pick you up tomorrow and we can go out to the beach," she replied.
"What time?" I asked.
"Eleven o'clock would be good. There is a tractor that takes people out to the bird sanctuary around the cliffs. I thought it would be fun to see it so we need to be there at noon," she replied with excitement in her voice.

This was going to be fine, as I had the protection of my temple garments.

In 1978, a temple garment was a one-piece, white cotton/polyester fabric, short sleeved, knee length union suit. Specially blessed squares of cloth covered each of the areas that were touched by the old women in the temple. Temple garments were only taken off the body while in the shower or while swimming. Washing them was to be done in private and by hand. No unworthy eyes should view temple garments if they are to remain sacred. When a pair wore out, there were special instructions of how to dispose of the garment and burn the squares. Every Mormon knew of how temple garments saved soldiers, missionaries and women from all kinds of harm and evil. Mother swore that it was her temple garments that saved her life from a car accident in which she rolled three times. Even the Lakota Sioux Indians had been influenced by the power of Mormon teachings and temple garments. The famous Ghost Shirts of the massacre at Wounded Knee were a derivative of missionary teachings to the Indians about the protective power of temple garments. History aside, wearing temple garments was not at all comfortable and in the summer they were nothing but sweat suits.

Regardless of the garment issue, being in a public space with Leah was not going to put me in any spiritual danger. I did not, however, want her coming to my flat, as I was fearful of nosey Sister Thornson and the ever-watchful eyes and ears of Inter-Morm.

> "Great, why don't I meet you at the corner of Napier and Howard Street. See you then." I replied.

The conversation closed and the floodgates holding drowned feelings sprang wide open.
God was testing me one more time.
Adversity builds character.
Faith sister. Faith.

The Hawkes Bay beaches and cliffs are astounding. Sitting on the end of the trailer with other tourists, Leah and I were behaving as if we were at a family reunion. Old times, jokes and stories flowed. We got off the trailer and headed for the climb across the ridge to the high point of the cliffs. Below us were thousands of sea birds of all kinds. The crash of ocean waves against the rocks and shrills of diving gulls filled the air. Sea breezes whipped across our faces as the majesty of New Zealand's raw natural beauty consumed us. We left the cliffs for the safety of the beach and the clatter of the tractor engine which slowly pulled us along the shore.

Halfway back we came to a stop.

"Come on Pip, we get off here," announced Leah, as if she were a bus driver.

We jumped off the back of the trailer and waved to our short-term friends.

"Leah, what are we doing? How are we going to get back?" I asked.

"No worries Pip. See that beach house under the cliffs over there. It's ours for the weekend," she replied pulling out a single key from her pocket.

"But Leah, I need to tell the Thornson family I won't be back for church tomorrow," I said in a state of minor panic.

Arguing with Leah would be a lost cause. Appealing to her sense of responsibility was always a better tactic.

"Yeah Pippa, I thought about that. No worries, Mani called them this afternoon to tell them you were away for the weekend and not to expect you back until tomorrow night," she said.

End of subject.

Being with Leah was heaven. Conversation flowed so easily and fears and worries melted away in an instant. The hours flew by in discussion, silence, memories, stories and heartfelt confessions. The sun set on the beach and the cabin was lit by one small candle. The curtains were drawn and the familiar rhythm of the waves sang their precious lullaby. Leah gave me her shirt to wear to bed. I changed in the toilet to protect my temple garments from view. The only bed in the room was a double bed against the wall with a sheepskin cover and crisp white sheets. Like giddy girls at a sleepover we both climbed on the bed and quickly got under the weight of the covers.

Gushing up from the deep passage of my heart core to the surface of my body were all of my feelings that told me we were far from girls on a sleepover. Once lovers our bonds of intimacy felt totally natural. We kissed each other's tears gently away and as we had so many times before and the night slipped away in the safety of our warm embrace.

Pacific light pierced through the weave of the thin window curtains. It was late, the tide was in and nature's rhythms gently brought us to consciousness. If time and place could stop we both wished we could wave a magic wand to make it so. To protect our re-entry into reality we gave no thought to the future and made no conversation. Inevitably, our weekend had to end. Inevitably, I had failed the test and as fast as she had appeared she once again disappeared to go back to Wellington. I had to go back to my flat in Hastings wondering how I could balance my head and my heart, my God and my desire, my feelings and my fiancé.

It was Monday. I had to be at the Thornson house for family home evening at 7pm. I had to talk to Keito in the knowing that I could be honest with him about the situation in the hope that we would be able to find a solution to bring balance. I knew he would help me if he knew my struggle. I knew he would understand if he knew my deepest feelings. This was going to be the first test for us as an eternal couple.

Walking in to the kitchen from the backdoor I was greeted with the glare of Sister Thornson and the stare of Bishop Childress. No one else was in the house.

> "Where were you last weekend?" she demanded.
> "That's really none of your business, Sister Thornson," I calmly replied.

I needed to talk to Keito.

> "Oh yes it is! I know where you've been. You were out at the cliffs in a cabin with that woman from Wellington. I've learned all about your unnatural relationship with

those girls! How dare you bring this filth into my house and what are doing with my son?" she exclaimed not wanting an answer.

Her questions had already been answered. Inter-Morm.
Bishop Childress stepped forward.

"Sister Gordon, we have two witnesses from the beach that saw you engaged in unbecoming behavior with a Maori woman. After my discussion with Bishop Merrick of Wellington, I am to suppose that it was Leah Mirangi, a woman that you are clearly intimate with. Given this knowledge it is my responsibility to summon you to a Bishop's Court this Saturday at one o'clock in my office. As your judge in Israel, I will evaluate your standing in the church. As a temple woman, you may expect the consequences of your actions this weekend to be severe. I suggest you get down on your knees and ask the Lord for forgiveness. Thank you for having me Sister Thornson. See you on Saturday Sister Gordon."

He left.
End of subject.

My re-entry into reality came without a parachute.
There was no escape from facing the Bishop's Court.
My knowledge of the gospel told me that I could be disfellowshipped or excommunicated for the crime of loving Leah. Being dis-fellowshipped would put me on membership probation that would put me on a strict regimen of weekly interviews, goal setting and eternal check marks until such a time the Bishop would allow restoration to full membership. Being dis-fellowshipped would also strip me of all of my responsibilities in the church as well as prohibiting me from speaking or leading the young adult activities.

Excommunication could also be an option. My name would be struck
from the records of the church and I would be condemned to Hell.
Excommunication was spiritual death, severance from all I knew, shunning by all I knew. I had studied the trials and tribulations of Mormon
saints who had been excommunicated. Like the murderers of Joseph
Smith, an excommunicated soul was cast out in every level of life and
on every level of living. Excommunicated members died terrible deaths,
alone without family or friend. For a fleeting second I remembered the
worms. The road back to the fold for an excommunicated member ran the
gamete of forever long to never. Family shame and Inter-Morm would
pummel the Gordon name. Surely, given all that I had sacrificed excommunication could not be an option. Besides, I had learned in spiritual
living class that there were only three things you can do to be excommunicated, a) commit adultery, b) murder someone and c) deny the power of
the priesthood. Spending a weekend with Leah was not on this list so it
was impossible that excommunication could ever happen.
End of subject.

Whatever the impending outcome, I was banned forever from the
Thornson household. I was distraught over the fact that I was not given
an opportunity to explain my relationship with Leah to Keito for I knew
that he had the capacity to understand my feelings and to gently guide
me back to the path of righteousness. I felt that I could be all in a wife that
was prescribed for me to be if I would be given the chance. I knew that I
could overcome the temptation and relationship with Leah if Keito loved
me as much as she did. I needed to fight for him and I needed him to fight
for us. I needed him to fight for me.

His mother had a different agenda. The moment Bishop Childress left the
house Sister Thornson turned into a fire-spitting dragon. Like my own
mother she was filled with the venom of condemnation that she spat at
me all the way down the long driveway to my car parked on the street.
Sister Thornson would be relentless in her campaign to distance herself
and her family from any association with me. Simply, I was to be erased.
And in this moment, like my father had done so many years ago, I turned

the engine over and sped off to the safety of my own shadow. I never saw Keito again.

Mother landed.
Inter-Morm had called and as this was a spiritual crisis she saw it as her duty to put me back on the right track. Mother always had the ability to kick me down a little more when I was already flailing in the gutter. She demanded I take a sick week from work so that I could become enveloped in prayers, fasting, scripture study and endless lectures from her. The concept that her daughter loved another woman was beyond her imagination. She blamed Leah for poisoning my heart and conspiring to take me to Hell. She blamed Leah for dragging me down into the gutter. There was no mention of the fact that I had allowed it, that I had wanted to go with Leah, that I was comfortable in all the love and new found freedom that she offered. There was no mention or discussion of my deepest feelings or how I came to this place in my life. Mother was convinced that I had no part in this ugliness. Mother was convinced that because I was a modern Mormon model of gospel perfection, Satan was working especially hard to take me on a detour to Hell. It was her job to pull me back. It was her mandated responsibility to save my soul.

Saving my soul was impossible. No one had the key to the matchbox so tightly closed in the corner of my heart filled with worms, dirty fingernails, kissing lessons, and no character. The little box had become huge. Over stuffed with sinful desires and prohibited wants the agony of its existence permeated all of my being. What would it take for me to empty its contents? What would it take for the burden of its weight to be lifted? Leah and Mani provided respite from its contents; acceptance, no judgment, loyalty and unconditional love. Mother provided nothing.

Saturday. One o'clock.
The Bishop's councilmen sat in silence with their bestowed, bowed heads turned toward the only desk in the room. Six white men, waiting for an inspired revelation from Bishop Childress, a ruddy-faced Welshman with ginger hair and short, scrubbed fingernails.

Centered in the room my eyes followed wood grain patterns in the front panel of the Bishop's desk. I nervously shifted on my seat. Six pairs of eyes darted to my chair as sounds of squeaking metal broke the silence in the room. Shielding myself from their glances, I felt my senses rest on the color of warm wood in their cold office. All around me were white walls blending with white shirts, the weight of stale air needing to escape through an open door and the annoying buzz of fluorescent lights trying to fill a room in desperate need of a window. A buoy bell of singular thought rang in my mind.
"Be still," it warned.

Again, I shifted on my seat.
Again, six pairs of eyes darted toward my chair as sounds of squeaking metal broke the silence in the room. My breathing began to labor, as familiar feelings of guilt and shame once again bored their tendrils into my heart. Bishop Childress looked up from his desk of prayer.

> "Sister Gordon, by the power and authority of the office that I hold, the Lord's judgment this day is that you be excommunicated from the Church of Jesus Christ of Latter Day Saints. From this day forth you are cast out of the sight of the Lord and out of the presence of his righteous souls until such a time when, through action and repentance, you may be able to earn your way back into the fold of the Lamb."

The center wood desk panel became out of focus and my voice screamed in my head. Cast out! Did God not see my sacrifice for him, my obedience to his laws? God is kicking me out? Did God not see my good works? Wait a minute! This has to be a mistake. I'm not an adulterer, a murderer or a priesthood denier! Did God not see my Little Toot courage and my Kiwi sacrifice? Did Jesus not tell God that I had shone my light for him? Maybe God heard my mother too often. Maybe she had told God that I was a bitch, a whore, evil and in the gutter. Maybe the Holy Ghost told God about my matchbox. That had to be it. God knew about the worms, the kissing lessons, dirty fingernails and my need for hugs.

The Bishop's voice snapped me back to the coldness of my seat.

> "Sister Gordon, by the power of the Melchezidek priest-
> hood and the authority of this court, the Lord has given
> unto me this instruction through the power of the Holy
> Ghost. God the Father and his son Jesus Christ have cast
> you out of their holy presence. Sister Gordon, the Lord
> has spoken. From this day forth the Holy Ghost will not
> abide within your evil soul. From this day forth you will
> become like a cork upon the ocean waves on which you
> will be forever tossed too and fro by the buffetings and
> power of Satan. These things I say unto you in the name
> of God the Father and his only begotten son Jesus Christ,
> Amen."

Six men repeated "Amen".
Six men cast their eyes to the floor and waited for my exit.
Silence.

Their door closed tight behind me.
Six men in white shirts had prayed over me.
The Bishop, God's judge in Israel, announced that God the Father and his
son Jesus Christ had cast me out of their presence because people like me
don't count in Heaven.
People like me don't belong in Heaven.
People like me don't belong.
Silence.

My entire world, all that I had withstood, all that I had understood,
imploded.

CHAPTER 16

MATTHEW 5:16

*"Let your light so shine before men, that
they may see your good works and
glorify your father in heaven."*

◇ ◇ ◇

Excommunication assures the sinner a front row seat in Perdition, a place of torment lower than Hell. The fact is the Mormon sinner who rejects Mormonism, the only true church of God, is worse off in the hereafter than someone who has never been taught the gospel. Simply, it would have been better if I had not been born at all.

Bishop Childress would now be required to announce my name and punishment to all priesthood holders in the Hastings Ward. He would also have to inform the general congregation, as part of Sunday school business notes. This ensured that Inter-Morm would spread the news of my excommunication to the entire Mormon population of New Zealand by late Sunday afternoon.

Shunning is taken very seriously in these matters, as Mormons have great respect for Satan's ability to influence the mind and body of righteous souls. Any association with evil spirits could become a spiritually dangerous and a risky game of righteous jeopardy. Therefore, the congregation was told to pray for me, and, at all cost, to disconnect from my evil self. My name was struck from the church records to ensure that no Mormon would ever make contact, and I was forbidden to speak in church or lead any young adult activities. Silence and silencing were to be my penance and punishment.

Mother drove me home, talking all the way. Her muttering became radio static in my ears. The decree of the Bishop's Court echoed through every cell in my brain. I don't remember what we ate for dinner or what time it was when she went upstairs to bed. Darkness enveloped me on the couch where, devoid of feeling, my eyes slowly closed. The pictures on my wall transformed into black shapes fading against the darkness of silence. I registered the corner television. Also silenced, it sat immovable and at an angle to the corner wall. My breath became heavy. Silence gave way to the thunder beat of my heart and the waves of rushing blood pumping through constricted arteries. At once I became aware of a large, masculine form that stepped out from the darkness of the wall below the stairs.

I could not move. Fear screamed at my body to move. Cloaked and hooded, he started to walk slowly towards me immobile on the couch. Again my brain ordered my body to sit up, raise my arms in defense, anything. I could not move. My chest expanded and contracted in pain. I fought for air. Eyes now fixed on the figure, my senses registered nothing but weight, mass, the pure essence of evil and horror in the recognition of it. It, who was it? His hood partially concealed a form void of eyes, expression or form. He has no face! He was close! Close enough to touch.

He began to push the weight of his world onto my chest. My silence screamed, "Get up! Get up! Get off the couch! I can't breathe!" He was so heavy. I couldn't move a muscle. My silence screamed, "I want to move! Sit up, sit up! Move! Get up!"

Death bent over my body and breathed his cold stench in my face. Without the protection of the Holy Ghost, Death had finally come to take me to Hell. My silent scream went unanswered, "Push him away! Save yourself! He's too big, he's too big! If you don't scream you are going to die!" I pleaded with my heart, "Voice, little voice, come out from your shadow." Nobody will see me.

I pleaded with my head, "Voice, little voice there is no need to hide." Nobody will find me.

I pleaded with my matchbox, "Voice, little voice, roar like your lion." Nobody will come.

Darkness and Death bent over my body to push Satan into my soul.

"Noooooooooooooo!!!!!!!," I shrieked out loud into the blackness of my living room.

My terrified scream shattered the silence of the night.

"Philippa, what's the matter?" my mother yelled from the top of the stairs. "Are you all right?"

The light switched on. My eyes were frantically scanning the room as I sat bolt upright on the couch gasping for breath.

> "What is it Philippa?" she asked again.
> "I thought someone was in here. Is anyone in the kitchen?" I asked.
> "No, now go back to sleep or you will be sick tomorrow," she replied.
> "Do you mind leaving the downstairs light on?" I asked.
> "Not at all. Good night Philippa."

I was not about to tell my mother what I had just experienced. She would use it as fodder to bolster her argument that my spiritual predicament was my fault and that clearly I needed to come home to be protected by the priesthood of my brothers. Her logic was terribly flawed. My brothers were bound to obey Mormon doctrine. Gospel principles dictated every decision, spiritual or secular. If my brothers acquiesced to familial proximity they would be heretics. They had no choice for their own salvation to shun me like everyone else, which they did. Decades would pass before any contact would be made.

In this night, sleep was not going to come. My eyes were too afraid to close. I was sure that if I closed my eyes Death would be back. I was sure the presence I felt was pure evil. I was sure my scream had foiled his attempt to consume my soul. I was sure that as a branded spiritual outcast, unworthy of God's protection or care, I had just received my first buffeting from Satan.

Sunrise came, then early morning. Mother began to stir upstairs, which was my signal to get up. She had insisted we go to church to show the Bishop I was going to do all I could to repent, starting today. I did not want to fight with her anymore and I knew that going to church would be fine if we could sit in the back un-noticed by judging eyes. I dressed for church, as I had dressed for church a thousand times before. I put on stockings and makeup for church, as I had done a thousand times before. Carrying my two large books of scriptures I headed out the door to church, as I had done a thousand times before.

We were late, so most of the pews had filled. Mother had the usher take us to the only pew that had space - second pew from the front.

"Let's go, Philippa. Hold your head up, you are still a Gordon," she said loudly.

We started down the aisle. The walk to the pew took forever. All eyes were upon us as we sat. Two large flashing electric signs, 'Lesbian' and 'Evil,' sat on each of my shoulders. A large pointer in the sky had an arrow to my head that said "Outcast." My eyes sought the floor and my head bowed low. I knew that, as this meeting was the third meeting of the day, the congregation had been told of my excommunication.

The service finally finished and we were ushered out of the pews. My young adult teacher looked away when I came near, as did everyone else I tried to make eye contact with. I walked over to my Sunday School teacher to say I was sorry and hoped that she would forgive me. Her hand became a stop signal in my face and she turned away in silence. I bit my lip to stop the tears and bolted for the front door for air. The shunning had begun.

I would have preferred it if Mother had been honest enough to just shave my head to get my humiliation out of the way. My understanding of public humiliation versus my mother's pride became clear. Taking me to church was all about holding high the 'Gordon' name. Mother would never stand for anyone to think that her children did not have the integrity and courage to do the right thing. Taking me to church had nothing to do with my feelings or my needs given the fact that my life, as I knew it, had just ended. Taking me to church was not about my salvation at all. I was furious and started to walk the five miles home. Mother caught up with me in the car and demanded that I get in.

"Philippa, what do you think you are doing?" she asked.

"Walking home," I replied with indifference.

"Don't use that snotty tone with me young lady, I am your Mother you know, and I have come all this way to help you," she said.

"Bullshit Mother! You only came to protect the Gordon name. You have no idea how much you've humiliated me in front of the Ward."

"Still have a filthy mouth I hear, and you were not humiliated, Philippa. You need to hold your head up high and not think about what others might think or say," she emphatically stated.

"Mother, that's so easy for you to say but you have no idea what it feels like to be excommunicated from the church!" I replied.

"Well Philippa, if the shoe fits, wear it. You have brought this all on yourself. I told you not to associate with those Maori girls and you ignored my advice. Now look at you. You're a Lesbian! You weren't born that way and you were certainly raised to know better! What you need to do is get down on your knees and pray for forgiveness every day until you repent," she scolded.

"What I need to do is get away from everyone to sort this out on my own. What I don't need is your continual criticism," I replied.

"Philippa, I am your Mother. It is my duty to teach you the gospel. You have no idea how much your behavior has hurt me and hurt your brothers! How do you think they feel when their friends come up to them and ask them if their little sister is unnatural with women! Disgusting, it makes me want to vomit. What did I do to deserve this? I gave you everything I could, especially the knowledge and truth of the gospel, and what do you do with it? What do you do with it? I'll tell you what you do with it. You throw it in the gutter, that's what you do with it. Going to church is the least that you can do for your mother, and it should be something you should be doing for yourself!

End of subject.
Mother left.

All I am was entwined with the gospel and its teachings. All I had become in life was built on Mormon foundations. Every fiber in my body had Mormon roots. Who am I if not a Mormon? What was I to become if I was barred from attaining Mormon perfection? Excommunication meant that God had taken all my blessings away. God had eradicated all my achievements and service to the church. God was so disappointed in me that he did not want to hear or listen to any of my prayers. God hated me so much that he did not want me in his presence. God had wrapped me up in white shirts and thrown me into the rubbish tin.

The following Thursday, there came a knock at my door.
It was Lindsay Morris from the Young Adult program. She had come to see if I needed anything. Expecting her to say no, I invited her in. Surprisingly, she stepped through the door and into my dining room.

> "How are you Pip? Are you holding up ok? I know what happened last weekend and I am so sorry for that," she said with such love.

My tears came and I had to wait to catch my breath to speak. She patiently sat in a kitchen chair to the sound of my sniffles. Gaining some composure I replied,

> "I'm sorry Lindsay, sorry for being such a mess."

"You have every right to be a mess, given what you've gone through," she replied.

Her answer was of some comfort.

> "Well Lindsay, I feel really down on the bottom right now. My heart is sore and my head is so confused I don't know what to think. I feel like cellophane you know, like if a breath of wind came I would blow away. Without the church I am nothing. I don't even know who I am anymore, which makes me feel like going down the rabbit hole."
>
> "What do you mean by that?" she asked with concern in her voice.
>
> "If I can't live with the church in my life I don't want to live at all," came my stilted reply.
>
> "Pip, don't talk stupid talk. You don't want to do that. Look, it's going to be all right, I promise. Look at all the people you have helped here. What can we do to help you?" she asked.
>
> "Nothing, nothing at all. Please Lindsay, you know you shouldn't even be around me. I'm not a good influence right now. I'm nothing anymore," I said sobbing into my tissue.
>
> "I don't believe that Pip. Look, I'm going to stay with you for a while to make sure that you don't do something dumb. Have you eaten today? Let's have some grub and some hot chocolate. That will make you feel better."

Tissues had rubbed my nose raw and tearstains marked my cheeks. I tried to eat but my appetite was non-existent. Lindsay helped me into bed and soon after she left, the fearful darkness of the night slowly crept up the stairs. How was I going to survive the night? I needed to keep awake, scan the room and look for shadows. But if I was to live, I had to be able to survive the night for thousands of nights to come. I jumped out of bed and ran for the light switch.

Light. I needed light. Satan never came in the light. I would learn to sleep with the light on. I closed the window shades in case Satan lurked outside my window. I opened my closet door to make sure nothing could take refuge there from the light. Paranoia replaced consciousness and fear became my unwelcome bedfellow. 'Faith, sister, faith,' no longer had any effect on the pain of my loss and the depth of my emptiness.

I quit my job.
I burned my temple garments as directed.
I gave the required one months notice to move out of my flat. I had no idea whether I was going back to Wellington or straight to Hell. Going down the rabbit hole was the only way I knew to stop the pain and agony of living with my shame. Although suicide was against God's laws, the thought of it gave me relief from the responsibility of having to know what to do next.
I couldn't pray. I couldn't think. I wouldn't feel. I began to think about how it would feel to become invisible.
Gone.
Dead.

I remembered that Monica's husband, Jon, had died once. Working with an oil company in Australia, Jon's job was to test the quality of crude oil by floating out on a platform over a three-foot pond of thick black gold. With another man to pull the rope, the two men traversed the oil ponds back and forth until testing was complete. One afternoon, the two men slipped on the raft and thumped down on the same side. The raft immediately flipped, trapping Jon and his coworker underneath it. The raft was too heavy for the men to lift and the wire ropes were too narrow for them to escape their cage.

Jon knew that he was going to drown. The pain in his lungs was commanding his brain to open his mouth to breathe so he resigned himself to death and calmly opened his mouth to let crude oil fill his lungs. He said there was no pain once he had made the hard decision. He arched his back, allowed his clenched mouth to open to breathe oil, at which point his spirit gently left his body to float above the scene. Thirty minutes later emergency workers lifted the raft off their bodies and pronounced them both clinically dead at the scene.

Australian law requires an attempt to resuscitate all drowning victims so Jon's body was taken to the emergency room, where they jammed a tube down his esophagus and sucked the black, thick crude out of his lungs. Fifteen minutes later they had a heartbeat. Jon was back. His co-worker was not so lucky.

I began to make a mental list of the ways I could die.
As Jon had said "drowning didn't hurt," I could rent a boat at the dock and row out to sea. I could jump in, the boat would float away, and I would tread water, waiting to sink. If I wore heavy clothes to weigh me down it wouldn't take long to sink to the bottom of the sea. But my pragmatic brain began to sabotage my thinking. Sharks could be a problem and, as I had seen the recently released movie of 'Jaws,' I had no desire to be ripped apart by the Great White sharks common to New Zealand waters. There had to be another way I could drown. I could drown myself in the bathtub, though that would mean finding something to keep my head under water and, what if the phone rang while I was under the water. If I blocked my ears with earplugs and found a brick to place on my chest – this was getting too complicated!

Gas. I had a gas stove and if I left the gas jets on full, I would simply fall asleep and eventually die. My problem-solving mind interrupted again. Lindsay might make the front door latch spark, which would cause my flat, and Lindsay, to explode. I had no desire to be in little pieces; if I was good enough to be resurrected, my body needed to be in one piece.

Cremation is prohibited in the Mormon Church, as God needs our bodies to be fully intact for the resurrection. My faith knew God created the planets, but logic challenged the notion that God could put together galaxies but he couldn't put together cremated bodies. I was compelled to obey these commandments, despite the fact that I believed cemeteries took too much space, being eaten by worms was disgusting, and waiting for the resurrection, while you rot six feet under, was a scenario too hellish to imagine. My only way out of this dilemma was the fact that as an excommunicated Mormon I was too evil to live the commandments with any kind of accountability. This was the only advantage to being out of the church, as come hell or high water I was going to be cremated.

Pills. If I swallowed a bottle of pills I would fall asleep and die. Then again, if Lindsay came over and saw the empty pill bottle she would call the ambulance and take me to the emergency room. There, they would shove a tube down my throat and pump the drugs out of my stomach. Like Jon, I would come back to life and back to lots of explaining to do. Suicide logistics were becoming ridiculous, a macabre series of action, reaction scenarios. The bottom line was that I didn't have the stomach for it, nor did I want to meet the Mormon God any sooner than I absolutely had too, especially in my excommunicated state of being.

I tried to rest my fractured brain. My heart was weary. From my nothing soul the words to my once favorite hymn quietly squeezed between my vocal chords,

> "...A-bide with me, 'tis eventide, the day is past and gone, the shadows of the evening fall, the night is coming on...O Savior, stay this night with me, behold tis eventide, O Savior, stay this night with me, behold tis eventide..."

I had learned the hymn in my Sunbeam class.

Sunbeam class.
I slowly whispered out my Sunbeam song,

> "...Jesus wants me for a Sunbeam, to shine for him each day, in every way try to please him, at school, at home, at play. A Sunbeam, a Sunbeam, Jesus wants me for ..."

I choked on the words and every voice in me retreated to silence.
Jesus didn't want to stay with me, my Sunbeam song was a lie, and suicide was not an option.

CHAPTER 17

MATTHEW 5:8

"Blessed are the pure in heart, for they shall see God."

1 979. An armada of small sailing vessels, along with the activist ship, 'Greenpeace,' sailed out to the mouth of Wellington Harbor to meet the American nuclear-powered aircraft carrier 'USN Enterprise' to stop her from entering port. On board this colossal war machine was the equivalent of the entire New Zealand Air Force, New Zealand Navy and New Zealand Coast Guard. Although intimidating, the sheer size of the ship never ruffled the defiant, principled Kiwi yachtsmen; the New Zealand Nuclear Free Zone would stand. Unable to maneuver past the courageous flotilla of hundreds of seaworthy craft, the 'USN Enterprise' stayed offshore in the outer banks. The stand-off proved to all that New Zealand was God's country, complete with a David and Goliath complex and a determination to be free of any nuclear arms. There was, however, a side note missed in the local press: the 'USN Enterprise' sat too deep in the water, a fact that prohibited her entry into the shallow, rock-strewn Wellington Harbor.

By August of the same year, the New Zealand National Health Care program and the National Railway System shared the honor of being the most inefficient services in the country; it took six months to secure a hospital room or bed and the trains were always late. The great Polynesian immigration had also started that year, with thousands of Samoans, Tongans, Fijians and Cook Islanders flooding into New Zealand for employment and a higher standard of living. Racial tensions began to escalate, as the Maoris asserted themselves as the top of the Polynesian social order, while they delegated the Samoans to the bottom. All other island groups were relegated somewhere in between. Consequently, ethnic pride ran rampant, gangs ruled neighborhoods, and knife and machete fights were common, especially after a night at the pub.

The New Zealand All Black rugby team was still boycotting apartheid South Africa and the New Zealand cricket team was still losing to the Pakistanis. National pride was devoutly aligned with the symbolic Kiwi black shirt with silver fern, and Olympic gold was gained in running the mile and the infamous Kiwi rowing eight's.

There were two television channels that broadcast from ten o'clock in the morning to eleven o'clock at night. The only exception to this schedule was live coverage of the English Soccer Cup final match, which usually started at two o'clock in the morning. School uniforms were still required through high school, and the language requirement for all children changed as often as New Zealand trading partners: Latin in the 1940's, French in the 1960's and Japanese in the 1970's. Due to the Maori Renaissance of the 1980's, today New Zealand is bilingual. The Maori language is finally required for nothing other than the survival of their indigenous culture and the reclaiming of their land and customs.

By September of 1979, inflation in New Zealand had risen eighteen percent. The cost of butter went up to from eighteen to twenty-six cents a pound, a bottle of milk went up from four to six cents a pint, and a side of butchered New Zealand lamb had raised in price to six dollars. This was outrageous given the fact that New Zealand had thirty million sheep. Travelers could fly the fifteen hundred miles to Sydney, Australia, for two hundred dollars or fly to Los Angeles, via Hawaii, for eight hundred dollars. The country went from a five-day working week to an unheard of six-day working week; until then New Zealand had been closed for the weekends. Hard working, middle class, single income families began to strain under high prices and low wages. Pakeha's, especially the baby boomer generation, began to immigrate to Australia for exactly the same reason Islanders were immigrating to New Zealand; a higher wage and more opportunities.

Leaving my flat in Hastings was difficult but necessary. I needed to travel light to be ready for whatever came next in my life. With no income and with the money from selling all my furniture, I moved into the screened in back porch of a little brown farmhouse in Bridge Pa, Hawkes Bay. Bridge Pa was a good thirty minutes drive from the city of Hastings and far enough away from Sister Thornson and Bishop Childress.

Rowena and I had met in the church Young Adult program in Hastings. Knowing the desperation of my situation she invited me stay until I had determined where to go. My friend Lindsay lived half a mile away, so all in all, the few friendly Mormon Maoris of Bridge Pa soon became my adopted support system.

Rawhinia was Rowena's grandmother who was eighty-four years old; a quiet, wise, humble and hard-working Maori woman, who still chopped her own firewood, had no indoor septic system, washed clothes by hand and cooked lamb heads and ham bones on the stove top. Each night I would leave the crackle of a warm fire to crawl under the weight of cold sheets and my large heavy sheepskin bed spread. It was late September and the Hawkes Bay winter was rainy and bone-numbingly damp. At first light I would emerge from the covers to see my warm breath turn to steam in the cold air. Lindsay often came over late at night to crawl under my covers, where, like schoolgirls, we would giggle and talk about our day. I would finally go to sleep resting on her shoulder. Her visits became quite regular and I depended on her to be the best hot water bottle in town, as she would cuddle closer and closer to me on every visit. I became nervous, and given the circumstances of my excommunication, I tried to be vigilant in keeping my physical distance.

Feeling humbled on all levels, I felt grateful to be welcomed by a forgiving family. I had no contact with my own family since Mother had left after my excommunication. Happy to be sleeping with a roof over my head I came to a new understanding of the story of the Good Samaritan every time I looked deeply into my newly adopted Maori grandmother's eyes. I knew that her kindness and generosity were the attributes of angels.

Rawhinia's house was devoid of rugs or carpet on the old pine floors, which made it cold on the feet, cold in the house and hard on Rawhinia's swollen, arthritic joints. Desiring to return their hospitality, I asked

Rowena if I could purchase carpet for the entire house. She was elated at the thought of warm wool under foot, so I arranged for the carpet to be purchased, delivered, and laid for a total cost of six hundred dollars, which I paid in cash from my savings. I never saw the carpet, as by the time it was installed, I was eight thousand miles away.

The previous year I had made inquiries to Brigham Young University, a Mormon school in Utah, about the possibility of attending the school as an international student. Paperwork and fees were sent abroad and I soon received notification I was accepted into the school, pending the necessary visa. Now, a year later, I realized that I would never be allowed entry to B.Y.U., given the fact that I was an excommunicated Mormon. Non-Mormons may attend the university, but deviants from the fold were turned away. Luckily, I had also made inquiries at the Rose Brueford School in London. This became another option and I began to consider the possibility of leaving New Zealand to follow my Plan A dream of working in the theater.

London was in the middle of the violent Pakistani race riots so the timing to go there was not ideal. America on the other hand was quite safe and any university program there would give me broader choices. The United States would also be a cheaper place to live. I would need at least two thousand dollars, eight hundred for the plane ticket and the rest for getting on my feet.

I had nothing to lose. Drama had always been my hobby, and as there was no theatre education program in New Zealand that offered a degree in the subject my only path was to go overseas. When I was young, my mother had taken me to see the English National Theatre's production of 'Snow White and the Seven Dwarfs'. I remember climbing hundreds of stairs to get to our cheap wooden benches closest to the ceiling. Despite the great distance from the stage, the production held my focus and opened my imagination. For weeks afterwards I would march around the house singing,

"...Hi ho, hi ho, it's off to work we go, hi ho, hi ho, hi ho, Hi ho,
hi ho, it's off to work we go, hi ho, hi ho, hi ho..."

Whenever I came upon a mirror I would stop to recite with a wicked tone and big nasty eyes,

"...Mirror, mirror, on the wall, who is the fairest of them all,
A-ha, ha, ha, ha, ha! (insert wicked witch cackle here)...."

Drama was definitely in my DNA.

My first Hamilton Community Theatre role was that of the Door Mouse in *'The Mad Hatter's Tea Party.'* At twelve years old, I was the Artful Dodger in the musical *'Oliver'* for a church production for the Hamilton Fourth Ward. The Director was Sister Hope Strong, a good friend of my mother's. She had recruited my mother for her ability as an interior decorator and to become a costume designer for the stage. As a consequence, Mother would drag me to every second-hand clothing store and every dusty costume rental warehouse in the area. I became a walking clotheshorse and note taker, all of which I detested, not to mention the stench of stale costumes from musty basement storage rooms. Nonetheless, my mother loved the work and it wasn't long before she and Hope Strong had founded the Hamilton Light Opera Club.

The first productions were Gilbert and Sullivan light operas such as *'The Mikado,' 'The Gondoliers,'* and 'The Pirates of *Penzance.'* By the third season, they were ambitious enough to produce *'The King and I,' 'West Side Story,'* and *'Hello Dolly.'* It was great fun. Mrs. Strong's husband, Cyrus, designed and built all the scenery. I was often his right hand help, painting hundreds of bricks for *'West Side Story,'* stealing fire extinguishers from church for the *'Hello Dolly'* steam train and painting miles of fabric for *'The King and I.'* By the time I was fifteen, I was smitten with the drama disease. Many afternoons after school were spent in rehearsal for school plays, church skits and community children's theatre.

Sister Strong had two daughters, Sarah, eighteen, and Violet, two years my junior. Hope would always ask me to attend activities with Violet, as she saw me as Violet's righteous example; I supposed from this that Violet was not as active in the church as Hope wanted her to be. My brothers were more interested than I was in Sarah and Violet, which meant that as a tag-along, I would always end up with them sitting in a tree hut, making plays in the living room or listening to *Jethro Tull* on Sarah's record player. By the time I was twenty, Violet was eighteen and well into the Disco and drug scene. Her boyfriend was not a Mormon and she would often take party trips with him to Australia without the knowledge or consent of her mother.

Desperate times required desperate measures and for Violet this meant she was shipped off to Utah to attend a Mormon school and hopefully meet and marry an upstanding Mormon Elder. Hope Strong's plan worked. By the time I was excommunicated, Violet was married in the Logan Temple in Utah to a local American returned missionary. Hope and my mother decided that a trip to Utah could do the same good for me. A message came through for me to phone Hope Strong as soon as possible. It was the first week of October 1979.

"Hello Sister Strong, this is Philippa. You asked me to call you," I said. "Yes, thank you for getting back to me so quickly Philippa, I've just received a letter from Violet in Utah. She's having such a great experience there. I hope you don't mind, but I told her of your difficulties in the church and she suggested you go to Utah to visit for a few weeks, just to get away for a holiday to sort your thoughts out. What do you think?" she asked, assuming I would jump at the opportunity.

"Well, I don't know, I mean, I really can't afford it and I certainly don't want to impose on Violet and her husband," I replied, hoping that my answer would end the subject.

But Hope was not going to be deterred from her mission.

"You know Philippa, you and Violet have been friends for a long time and you've always been such a good example to her. Cyrus and I have been so thankful that you've helped her through her tough times, so we just want to help you in some way by returning the favor," she said.

What Hope didn't know was that I despised Violet and viewed her as a spoiled, entitled girl who had little character. I was also very tired of being delegated the job of "being the good example" to Violet. I had lied on her behalf, lost money on her behalf and was generally used as a convenient rescuer when Violet would get herself into dangerous situations with men or drugs. It was Violet who owed me, not her parents.

"Well Hope, I was happy to help out when I could, but I need to look at my own problems now," I replied.
"You know, I understand that but Cyrus and I would like to pay for a round-trip plane ticket to Utah," she stated.

I was stunned to silence.
Why would Hope be willing to pay my way to Utah?
Why was she being so persistent?

"That's very thoughtful of you both. I'll think about it for a day or two and get back to you," I said, stalling for time.

Decisions were really hard to make anymore.

"Yes, of course Philippa, but please accept our offer. Violet will be delighted to see you as she's terribly homesick and needs a good friend like you to visit. Get back to me soon. Bye-bye Philippa."

She hung up.

And there it was.
Hope always an agenda and always had an ulterior motive.

Violet was homesick and needed someone to visit her. I should have known there was another reason, other than my well being, for Hope to push me to visit. Hope was so manipulative and I always fell into her traps. When would I learn that her concern was always going to be for Violet, not for me. This offer was par for the course; I was needed to go over to the States and rescue poor, homesick Violet.

Hope's motives became even more transparent when I received a letter from my mother in the same week in which she planted the idea that, "...as I was at a crossroad in my life, I might take an opportunity to travel..." Hope and Mother were conniving together to get me away from my Maori friends in Bridge Pa and off to the very cornerstone and hub of Mormonism: Salt Lake City, Utah. Their plot was to have me go to America, get reinforced in Mormon righteousness, and then return to Auckland to continue my righteous path under Inter-Morm and Mother.

That night I shared my frustrations and hurts about the Mother/Hope plots with Lindsay. She thought it was a great idea for me to travel, especially if they were willing to pay for it. We talked about my desire to study abroad. It occurred to both of us it would be easy to go to Utah on a tourist visa, enroll in the nearest university and change my visa to a student visa for the duration of my studies. What a great idea! I called Hope the next day and accepted her offer. She wired me the money for the plane ticket the following day.

With my ticket purchased and my tourist visa obtained, I was set to leave Auckland two and a half weeks later on October 29, 1979. Days passed so quickly I had no time to back out of the plan. I gave Lindsay my sheepskin bedspread and pillow. This left me with a small suitcase for clothes, scriptures, two high school yearbooks and a photo album. I packed an orange rental car and got ready to drive the two hundred miles to Auckland the following day.

My last night with my Maori grandmother was spent in front of a raging fire. Hugs and blessings were shared, evening prayers were offered and we all went to bed knowing I would be up and off at six o'clock in the morning. I drove away from Bridge Pa as the morning mist began to lift from the tall green grass and the little brown house I had come to love. I imprinted the picture in my mind's eye, knowing the memory of my refuge would have to last.

Auckland International Airport was eerily quiet for eight o'clock at night. I sat on the lobby bench with my boarding pass and ticket in hand. My sister Rebecca had come with my Mother to see me off. I had not seen her in so long but there was no time or space for me to catch up on her life. Rebecca was very quiet; she was thinking of all the times Mother had stopped her from going to America. Her resignation showed in her sad expression as she watched me act out her dream - her dream to get away. Her dream extinguished so many husbands and bruises ago.

Monica, Jon and their two older children were there to see me off. They had not seen me since my excommunication, and were generally concerned about my wellbeing. I was touched they came, as it was nice to see friendly faces whose only agenda were to wish me safe travels. My brother Cedric was there for reasons I know not. His presence was only a reminder of the shame and the secrets still stuffed tightly into that little matchbox in the corner of my heart.

Mother was calm in her assured knowledge from my return ticket that I would be back in three weeks. What she didn't know was this was the moment of my great escape: my escape from Inter-Morm, my escape from family expectations, my escape from the shunning and the shaming, my escape from the prying questions of Bishops, my escape from men and fiancés in white shirts and spotless souls, my escape from the cruel Moon and secrets.

My international flight number for the British Airways jumbo jet was called over the Intercom. My sister immediately started to cry; every tear her unspoken wish that she could go with me. My hug enveloped her broken frame and beaten spirit. She slipped a New Zealand twenty-dollar bill in my pocket.

"I thought you might need a bit of change to get you through the airport. Sorry it can't be more," she whispered in my ear.
"No worries sis," I said holding her close, "I'll send some American stuff back for you and the kids once I get on my feet."

She slid back into the curve of the plastic airport chair.
I could not save her.
I could only save me.

Monica and Jon wished me the best and made sure I had sunscreen in my luggage. I did. Hugs and handshakes were given all around, then the turn to face Mother who had been waiting to be last in the sendoff line.

"So, Philippa, send me a postcard when you land. I have been in touch with the Bishop in Logan so they are expecting you at church on Sunday. Have a good flight."
"Goodbye Mother."

She did not offer hugs or healing, handshakes or joy.
My leaving was just another day, just another flight, just another goodbye, and just another "see you later." What she did not know was that I was determined never to see her later. I was going to do everything in my power to never come back. I was going to do everything in my power to find a life without the admonitions of the Mormon Church and Mother.

I turned to join my fellow passengers in the very long line to the hostess taking tickets at the jet-way. My stomach filled with butterflies and my thoughts were spinning as fast as the jet turbines now warming up to fly. I took my first step forward in the line.

My feelings were hurt at my mother's cold countenance. Here I was going on the trip of a lifetime and she could not muster one word of joy or one hug of comfort. As usual her only concern was to get me to the office of the next Bishop. She had always been this way. There was never any celebration in our house; no birthdays, no toys, no Christmas presents, no Easter eggs, no parties, no movies, no friends, no safety, no joy. There was only work and secrets. I felt tired and I wasn't even on the plane yet. I shuffled forward in the line.

I had worked hard for my family's approval. The harder I worked, the more elusive their approval became. So, as I was taught, I worked harder, sacrificed more, trusted more, and gave more. Approval never came and betrayal was my reward. My brothers and my Mormon God told me I was invisible. My mother and my Mormon God showed me that my life did not matter and my work did not count. God rejected my Sunbeam, and like Mrs. Cheverton had done so early in my life, God also threw me into the dog kennel to live with the shadows on the wall.
I shuffled forward in the line.

I wondered if this was how my father felt. Perhaps he had left that rainy night so long ago because, like me, he couldn't breathe anymore. Like me, he felt alone in the sea and rip tides of Mother and the Mormon Church. Like me, the harder he worked for my mother's love, the more she withheld it. To her, love was a noun instead of a verb. In her Mormon mind and heart to speak, "I love you" was enough. But it wasn't enough. I needed attention and I needed acceptance from a mother who would love me even though I was not perfect. I would never be perfect. I was drowning in the pursuit of it and my only lifelines were ripped from my grasp.
I shuffled forward in the line.

Leah and Mani loved me for anything and everything I wanted to be, without judgment, without shame. I could talk to them about anything and I so wished they were here at the airport to see me off. I missed them so much. I needed to sit and talk about who I was and what it was that I needed. I needed to laugh. I needed to cry. I needed a sense of self worth that was not tied to my performance in the church. I didn't need job lists and speech assignments. I needed a hug.
I shuffled forward in the line.

My mother's mantra was always *"blood is thicker than water."* The fact that we all had the same blood running through our veins was all we needed to know. She would often scoff at the absurdity of my thinking. Her answer to doubt was always,"...of course we love you Philippa, what a silly question. We are your family and blood is thicker than water, you know. Nothing will change the fact that we are a family. Ask your brother's; they will tell you that they love you. Really, how ridiculous to ever think they wouldn't. Did those Maori girls put that thought into your head?" Silence.
I shuffled forward in the line.

Love as a noun is inactive, a four-letter little word; a lie if you say it too often and a tragedy if you only hear the word but never feel it. I needed love to be a verb, a doing word. I needed to be nurtured, held and valued, I needed to hear my family was proud of who I was. But first, I needed to figure out who I was and I would have to do it entirely on my own. This I was determined to do and my ticket to America, the Promised Land, was the ticket that would give me the freedom to navigate my life without their boundaries. I was determined to work as hard as I had ever worked to follow my own dream; a dream without Death, a dream without worms and dirty fingernails, a dream without guilt and a dream without betrayal. I gave the boarding pass to the hostess and began to walk down the ramp to the door of the plane.

It took twenty minutes to load the passengers and the luggage on the plane. The cabin air became still, the jet engines began to whine.
Seat 29A.
I pulled the buckle tight on my seatbelt.
The plane jerked and reversed out of the bay, turned and began to taxi to the runway. This was it.
I thought of my Kiwi courage.
This was my beginning.
I thought of my lion heart.
This was my great escape.
I thought of my matchbox in desperate need of light.
The plane swung around to face the length of the runway.

Turbines screamed, wing flaps groaned with extension, the terminal blurred.

Velocity pressed my being against the back of my seat.

Nose up.

Wheels up.

Lift off.

ACKNOWLEDGMENTS

In 2002 I sent my memoir to over 25 publishers and agents. At that time most sent me back polite rejections, many citing the fact 'they did not want to go up against the Mormon Church.' In 2011 the *Book of Mormon* opened on Broadway and Mormon Governor Mitt Romney ran for President of the United States. These two events brought Mormon culture and doctrine to the forefront of social media and the mainstream press. Finally the fear of going up against the Mormon church eroded so that our stories, and there are many, can finally come to light.

I am grateful for friends and colleagues who have endured, encouraged, inspired and read these pages since 2002. They weave the quilt in the writing and journey of this book. Molly Beth Griffin, my student who fervently made grammar corrections and style notes; now an author herself and an advocate, still. Authors, Christina Baldwin and Ann Lenea, authors both who held the power of inspiration and penmanship through multiple workshops on Whidbey Island; founders of PeerSpirit Inc, an amazing organization for the empowerment of women and enlightenment on the planet. I came to them as a little bird not sure of her wings… they taught me how to fly.

I have been fortunate to be in the company of friends who shaped my world; Rod, Leonard and Paul, Dan and Linda, all who taught me the artist way, Charlotte, Bobbie and Shirley, Jeff and Pat, Erik and Bill, whose encouragement has never ceased, Laura whose fierce voice made sure I would not silence my own, Becky and Cynthia, Sue and Annie, Roberta and Judy and the other women of Grinnell. I am grateful for the women of the Marshalltown book club who were so kind to read and critique my work in the safety of circle practice. I learned so much from their notes. I am thankful to author and screenwriter, Carolyn Briggs and several professional editors who could not print my manuscript but whose notes and letters gave encouragement and validation to the strength of my story. I am forever indebted to my spirit guides Josephine, Jeannine and Jan who agreed to begin the smallest of writing groups to encourage me to finish. Thanks also to Karn, Mox and Linda, Mary and Tom, Diana and Dave, Vicki and Chuck, Denise in Louisiana and last but not least, Nancy for being the consummate typo catcher and guardian. I am deeply grateful to the many friends and colleagues who are not named but who have walked with me for a spell on this creative journey.

Finally, to my students of Grinnell College who are now all working professionals in a myriad of fields; thank you for your lessons and lives lived with courage. And hope.

Pip Gordon
Marshalltown, Iowa
May 2013

.

Made in the USA
San Bernardino, CA
14 December 2013